Best Garden Plants *for* Oklahoma

Steve Owens • *Laura Peters*

Lone Pine Publishing International

The Distributor: Lone Pine Publishing
1808 B Street NW, Suite 140
Auburn, WA, USA 98001
Website: www.lonepinepublishing.com

Library and Archives Canada Cataloguing in Publication

Owens, Steve, 1966-
    Best garden plants for Oklahoma / Steve Owens, Laura Peters.

Includes index.
ISBN-13: 978-976-8200-30-3

    1. Plants, Ornamental--Oklahoma. 2. Gardening--Oklahoma.
I. Peters, Laura, 1968- II. Title.

SB453.2.O45O94 2007   635.909766   C2006-903712-4

Photography: All photography by Tamara Eder, Derek Fell, Tim Matheson, Alison Penko and Laura Peters except: AAFC 111b; AAS selection 23a; William Adams 102; Bailey Nurseries 120b; Steve Baskauf 144a, 144b; Pam Beck 166a, 166b; Sandra Bit 77a, 91a; Brendan Casement 85b; Janet Davis 111a; Joan de Grey 19b; Don Doucette 95b; Erika Flatt 15a, 125a; Anne Gordon 63b, 89a, 89b; Saxon Holt 38a, 38b, 46a, 75a, 75b, 76a, 76b, 77b, 129b, 157a, 157b, 158; Staci Jenkins 108b; Duncan Kelbaugh 125b; Liz Klose 155a, 164a, 165a, 165b; Debra Knapke 37a; Janet Loughrey 121a; Kim O'Leary 8, 12b, 24a, 26a, 26b, 37b, 78a, 78b, 92b, 118a, 118b, 123a; Photos.com 149a; Robert Ritchie 40b, 47a, 84a, 84b, 94a, 135a; Gene Sasse and Weeks Roses 110; Joy Spurr 112a; Dan Tenaglia 87a, 87b, 163a; Texas Cooperative Extension 108a; Peter Thompstone 18b, 20a; Mark Turner 46b, 81a, 81b, 104, 120a, 151b; Valleybrook Gardens 54a, 163b; Don Williamson 126a, 126b, 131a; Tim Wood 99a.

PC: P13

Table of Contents

Introduction

Starting a garden can seem like a daunting task, but it's also an exciting and rewarding adventure. With so many plants to choose from, the challenge is to decide which ones will work best here in Oklahoma. This book is intended to give beginning gardeners the information they need to start planning and planting gardens of their own. It includes a wide variety of plants and provides basic plant descriptions, planting and growing information and tips for use. With this book in hand, you can begin to produce a beautiful and functional landscape in your own yard.

Oklahoma is often divided into two distinct sections: Eastern and Western. However, dividing the state into four distinct gardening regions better represents the challenges gardeners face throughout the state. These regions are the High Plains (the Panhandle), the Arid Southwest (southwestern Oklahoma), the Continental East (the northeastern counties) and the Humid South (southeastern Oklahoma).

Oklahoma is a transition state. In the east we have the western edge of the Eastern Deciduous Forest with such plants as native azaleas and bald cypress, while in the west we have the beginning of the lower Great Plains, with Cholla cactus and sandsage artemesia. The interface area between the two regions is known as the Crosstimbers. Oklahoma has 11 level III ecoregions, each with its own unique set of challenges and advantages to growing certain plants with success.

The summer growing season is mostly hot and dry except in the eastern regions, which can be quite humid. Frost-free day averages range anywhere from 175 to 235 during the growing season. The winters are generally mild and short, and they are cold enough to ensure a good period of dormancy and plenty of flowers in spring. Rainfall is fairly unpredictable and most of the precipitation takes place in spring, with periods of drought occurring in both summer and winter. It is interesting to note that for every 15 miles on average that you travel from west to east, you get another inch of rainfall per year. The western part of the state is windier, so the moisture received doesn't hang around as long. It's not unheard of to see gardeners watering on a warm winter day in an effort to protect their gardening endeavors. The soil in Oklahoma, though not without its challenges, supports a variety of healthy plants and is alkaline in the west and acidic in the east.

Hardiness zones and frost dates are two terms often used when discussing climate and gardening. Hardiness zones are based on the minimum possible winter temperatures. Plants are rated according to the zones in which they grow successfully. The last frost date in spring combined with the first frost date in fall allows us to predict the length of the growing season and gives us an idea of when we can begin planting.

Microclimates are small areas that are generally warmer or colder than the surrounding area. Buildings, fences, trees and other large structures can provide extra shelter in winter but may trap heat in summer, thus creating a warmer microclimate. The bottoms of hills are usually colder than the tops but may not be as windy. Take advantage of these areas when you plan your garden and choose your plants; you may even grow out-of-zone plants successfully in a warm, sheltered location.

Getting Started

When planning your garden, start with a quick analysis of the garden as it is now. Plants have specific requirements, and it is best to put the right plant in the right place rather than to try to change your garden conditions to suit the plants you want.

Knowing which parts of your garden receive the most and least amounts of sunlight will help you choose the proper plants and decide where to plant them. Light is classified into four basic groups: full sun (direct, unobstructed light all or most of the day); partial shade (direct sun for about half the day and shade for the rest); light shade (shade all or most of the day with some sun filtering through to ground level); and full shade (no direct sunlight). Most plants prefer a specific amount of light, but many can adapt to a range of light levels.

Hardiness Zones Map

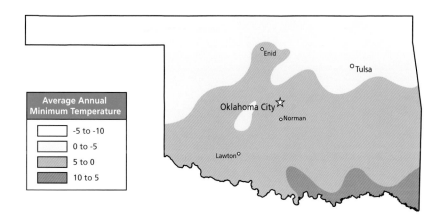

Soil is the foundation of a good garden. Plants use the soil to hold themselves upright and rely on the many resources it contains: air, water, nutrients, organic matter and a host of microbes. The soil particle size influences the amount of air, water and nutrients the soil can hold. Sand, with the largest particles, has a lot of air space and allows water and nutrients to drain quickly. Clay, with the smallest particles, is high in nutrients but has very little air space. Water is therefore slow to penetrate clay and slow to drain from it.

Soil acidity or alkalinity (measured on the pH scale) influences the amount and type of nutrients available to plants. A pH of 7 is neutral; a lower pH is more acidic. Most plants prefer a soil with a pH of 5.5–7.5. Soil-testing kits are available at most garden centers, and soil samples can be sent to testing facilities for a more thorough analysis that will give you an idea of which plants will do well in your soil and what amendments your soil might need.

Compost is one of the best and most important amendments you can add to any type of soil. Compost improves soil by adding organic matter and nutrients, introducing soil microbes, increasing water retention, increasing nutrient holding capacity and improving drainage. You can purchase compost, or you can make it in your own backyard.

Selecting Plants

It's important to purchase healthy plants that are free of pests and disease. Such plants will establish quickly in your garden and will not introduce problems that may spread to other plants. You should have a good idea of what the plant is supposed to look like—its habit and the color and shape of its leaves—and then inspect the plant for signs of disease or insect damage before buying it.

The majority of plants are grown in containers or nursery pots. This is an efficient way for nurseries and greenhouses to grow plants, but when plants grow in a restricted space for too long, they can become pot bound with their roots densely encircling the inside of the pot. Avoid purchasing plants in this condition; they are often stressed and can take longer to establish. It is often possible to temporarily remove the pot to look at the condition of the plant roots. You can check for soil-borne insects, rotten roots and girdling or pot-bound roots at the same time. Roots that are wrapped densely around the inside of a pot must be lightly pruned or teased apart before planting.

Planting Basics

The following tips apply to all plants.

• Prepare the garden before planting. Remove weeds, make any needed amendments and dig or till the soil in preparation for planting if you are

Gently remove container.

Ensure proper planting depth.

Backfill with soil.

starting a new landscape. The prepared area should be the size of the plant's mature root system.

- Settle the soil with water. Good contact between the roots and the soil is important, but if you press the soil down too firmly, as often happens when you step on it, you can cause compaction. This reduces the movement of water through the soil and leaves very few air spaces. Instead, pour water in as you fill the hole with soil. The water will settle the soil evenly without allowing it to compact.

- If the soil is heavy and sticky after a spring snowstorm or rainfall, wait until it dries out and becomes crumbly again before working it.

- Unwrap the roots. It is always best to remove any container to give the roots the chance to spread out naturally when planted. If the rootball is firm enough and will remain solid without support, the container can be removed before the plant is placed into the planting hole. If the rootball is not solid, the container should only be removed after the plant is properly placed and is supported by surrounding soil; otherwise, during transplanting, soil will fall away bringing with it some of the tender feeder roots. In particular, you should remove plastic containers and fiber pots from plants and wire and burlap from the top of the rootball when planting trees. Fiber pots decompose very slowly, if at all, and they wick moisture away from the plant. Synthetic burlap doesn't decompose, and wire will eventually girdle or strangle the roots as they mature. The peat pots and pellets used to start annuals decompose more readily and can be planted with the young transplants. Even these peat pots should be sliced down the sides, and any part of the pot that will be exposed above ground should be removed to prevent water from being wicked away from the roots.

- Accommodate the rootball. As a general rule, the size of the planting hole should be least two times the width of the rootball but no deeper than its height. If the rootball is planted too deeply, the plant will have a difficult time and may even die. The top surface of the rootball should be level with a fraction of an inch below the surrounding soil but no deeper. Tender roses are the only exception to this rule.

- Know the mature size of your plants. You should space your plants based on how big the plants will be when they are mature, rather than how big they are when you plant them. For example, a shrub that will grow to be 10' tall and wide may only be 12" when you buy and plant it. Large plants should have enough room to mature without interfering with walls, roof overhangs, power lines, walkways and surrounding plants.

Settle backfilled soil with water.   Water the plant well.   Add a layer of mulch.

- Identify your plants. Keep track of what's what in your garden by putting a tag next to each plant when you plant it. A gardening journal is also a great place to list the plants you have and where you've planted them. It is very easy, for beginning and seasoned gardeners alike, to forget exactly what they planted and where they planted it.

- Water deeply. It's better to water deeply when necessary than to water lightly more often. Deep and thorough watering forces roots to grow as they search for water and helps them survive dry spells when water bans may restrict your watering regime. Always check the rootzone before you water, because some soils hold more water for longer periods than other soils. Mulching helps retain moisture and reduces watering needs. Containers and container gardens are the watering exception, because they can quickly dry out and may even need watering every day.

Choosing Plants

Features such as decorative fruit, variegated or colorful leaves and interesting bark provide interest when plants aren't

Begonias and boxwood in a formal planting.

blooming. When choosing your plants aim for a selection with a variety of sizes, shapes, textures, bloom times and other features. A well-planned garden that includes plants with a diversity of attributes captivates your attention year-round.

Annuals

Annuals are newly planted each year and are only expected to last for a single growing season. Their flowers and decorative foliage provide bright splashes of color and can fill in spaces around immature trees, shrubs and perennials.

Annuals are easy to plant and are usually sold in small cell-packs of four or six plants. The roots quickly fill the space in these small packs, so the small rootball should be broken up before planting. Split the ball in two up the center or run your thumb up each side to break up the roots.

Many annuals are grown from seed and can be started directly in the garden once the soil has begun to warm up.

Perennials

Perennials grow for three or more years. They usually die back to the ground each fall and send up new shoots in spring, though they can also be evergreen or semi-shrubby. They often have a shorter period of bloom than annuals but require less care.

Many perennials benefit from being divided every few years, usually in early spring while plants are still dormant or, with some plants, after flowering. This keeps them growing and blooming vigorously, and in some cases controls their spread. Dividing involves digging the plant up, removing dead debris, breaking the plant into several pieces using a sharp knife, spade or saw and replanting some or all of the pieces. Extra bits can be shared with family, friends and neighbors.

Roses are lovely on their own or in mixed borders.

Trees & Shrubs

Trees and shrubs provide the bones of the garden. They are often the slowest growing plants but usually live the longest. Characterized by leaf type, they may be deciduous or evergreen, and needled or broad-leaved.

Trees should have as little disturbed soil as possible at the bottom of the planting hole. Loose dirt settles over time, and sinking even an inch can kill some trees. The prepared area for trees and shrubs needs to be at least two to four times wider than the rootball.

Staking, sometimes recommended for newly planted trees, is only necessary for trees over 5' tall. Stakes support the rootball until it grows enough to support the tree. Stakes should allow the trunk to move with the wind and should only remain in place for up to one year.

Pruning is more often required for shrubs than for trees, and even then, only dead or diseased wood should be removed. A woody plant is often pruned to control its growth when it is planted in a location that won't allow for its mature size. Pruning should never be used for this reason, and this situation can be avoided by researching what tree and shrub is best for a location based on space and light, etc. Pruning can be a benefit to fruiting trees, however, as well as to some flowering trees and shrubs.

Roses

Roses are beautiful shrubs with lovely, often fragrant blooms. Traditionally, most roses bloomed only once in the growing season, but new varieties bloom all, or almost all, summer. Repeat-blooming, or recurrent, roses should be deadheaded to encourage more flower production. One-time bloomers should be left in place for the colorful hips that develop.

Generally, roses prefer a fertile, well-prepared planting area. A general rule is to prepare an area at least twice the width of the rootball or a minimum of 24" in width for bare-root roses. Add plenty of compost or other fertile organic matter, and keep the roots well watered during the growing season. Many roses are quite durable and will adapt to poorer conditions. Grafted roses should be planted with the graft just above the soil line. When watering, avoid getting water on the foliage to reduce the spread of blackspot.

Roses, like all plants, have specific pruning requirements. Consult with your local extension department or garden center for specific information pertaining to pruning your roses.

Vines

Vines or climbing plants are useful for screening and shade, especially in a location too small for a tree. They may be woody or herbaceous, and annual or perennial. Vines may cling to surfaces, may have wrapping tendrils or stems, or may need to be tied in place with string.

Sturdy trellises, arbors, porch railings, fences, obelisks, pergolas, walls, poles and trees are all possible vine supports. If a support is needed, ensure it's in place before you plant the vine to avoid disturbing the roots later. Choose a support that is suitable for the vine you are growing. The support needs to be sturdy enough to hold the plant up and should match the growing habit of the vine—whether clinging, wrapping or tied.

Bulbs, Corms & Tubers

These plants have fleshy, underground storage organs that allow them to survive extended periods of dormancy. They are often grown for the bright splashes of color their flowers provide. They may flower in spring, summer or fall. Each has an ideal depth and time of year at which it should be planted.

Hardy bulbs can be left in the ground and will flower every year. Some popular, tender plants are grown from bulbs, corms or tubers and are generally lifted or removed from the soil in late summer or fall as the foliage dies back. They are stored in a cool, frost-free location over winter and are replanted in spring.

Herbs

Herbs are plants with medicinal, culinary or other economic purposes. A few common culinary herbs are included in this book. Even if you don't cook with herbs, the often-fragrant foliage adds its aroma to the garden, and the plants can be quite decorative in form, leaf and flower. A conveniently placed container of your favorite herbs—perhaps located near the kitchen door—will yield plenty of flavor and fragrance all summer.

Many herbs have pollen-producing flowers that attract butterflies, bees, hummingbirds and predatory insects to your garden. Predatory insects feast on problem insects, such as aphids, mealybugs and whiteflies.

Ferns, Grasses & Groundcovers

Many plants are grown for their decorative foliage rather than their flowers. Ornamental grasses, ferns, groundcovers and other foliage plants add a variety of colors, textures and forms to the garden. Many of these plants are included in other sections of this book, but we have set aside a few for the unique touch their foliage, form and habit adds to the garden.

Ferns provide a lacy foliage accent and combine attractively with broad-leaved perennials and shrubs. Ferns are common in moist, shady gardens but some selections will also thrive in the sunshine.

Ornamental grasses and grass-like plants provide interest throughout the year when the withered blades are left to stand all winter. They are cut back in early spring and divided when the clumps begin to die out in the centers.

Plants used for groundcovers are often vigorous, spreading or procumbent. These types of plants are frequently used as an alternative to grass, as a living mulch around the base of other, taller plants, to prevent erosion or purely for decorative purposes.

A Final Comment

The more you discover about the fascinating world of plants—whether from reading books, talking to other gardeners, appreciating the creative designs of others or experimenting with something new in your own garden—the more rewarding your gardening experience will become. This book is intended as a guide to germinate and nurture your passion for plants.

Angelonia
Angelonia

A. angustifolia (above & below)

With its loose, airy spikes of orchid-like flowers, angelonia makes a welcome addition to any garden.

Growing

Angelonia prefers **full sun** but tolerates a bit of shade. The soil should be **fertile, moist** and **well drained**. Although this plant grows naturally in damp areas, such as along ditches and near ponds, it is fairly drought tolerant. Plant out after the chance of frost has passed.

Tips

Added to an annual or mixed border, angelonia looks most attractive when planted in groups. It is also well suited to a pondside or streamside planting.

Recommended

A. angustifolia is a bushy, upright plant with loose spikes of flowers in varied shades of purple. Cultivars with white or bicolored flowers are available including **Angelface Series** and the **Angelmist Series**.

The individual flowers look a bit like orchid blossoms, but angelonia is actually in the same family as snapdragons.

Also called: angel wings, summer snapdragon **Features:** attractive purple, blue, white or bicolored flowers **Height:** 12–24" **Spread:** 12"

Begonia
Begonia

B. Rex Cultorum hybrids 'Escargot' (above)
B. semperflorens (below)

With their beautiful flowers, compact habit and decorative foliage, begonias are sure to fulfill your shade-gardening needs.

Wax begonias are ideal flowers for the lazy gardener because they are generally pest free, and they bloom all summer, even without deadheading.

Growing

Light or **partial shade** is best for these plants, though some wax begonias tolerate sun if their soil is kept moist. The soil should be **fertile, rich in organic matter** and **well drained** with a **neutral or acidic pH**. Allow the soil to dry out slightly between waterings.

Begonias love warm weather, so don't plant them out before the soil warms in spring. If they sit in cold soil, they may become stunted and fail to thrive.

Tips

All begonias are useful for shaded garden beds and planters.

Wax begonias have a neat, rounded habit that makes them particularly attractive as edging plants. Rex begonias, with their dramatic foliage, are useful as specimen plants in containers and beds.

Recommended

B. **Rex Cultorum Hybrids** (rex begonias) are grown for their dramatic, colorful foliage.

B. semperflorens (wax begonias) have pink, white, red or bicolored flowers and green, bronze, reddish or white-variegated foliage.

Features: pink, white, red, yellow, orange, bicolored or picotee flowers; decorative foliage
Height: 6–24" **Spread:** 6–24"

Blue Daze
Evolvulus

*A*ny plant with blue or purple-blue flowers has been all the rage for quite some time now, and for good reason. The cool colors are the perfect contrast to the super-trendy yellow and chartreuse foliage and flowering cultivars on the market.

Growing
Blue daze prefers to grow in **full sun** but tolerates light to partial shade. The soil should be **well drained** and of **poor to moderate fertility**.

Tips
Blue daze works beautifully in a decorative container and in a mixed bed or border. It carries the most punch when planted next to plants with fiery-colored flowers or foliage. Blue daze is quite stunning in a hanging basket.

Recommended
E. glomeratus is a trailing perennial that is often grown as an annual. It produces dark, tender stems that have dark green leaves with a touch of silvery sheen. The solitary, open-faced flowers are bell shaped and face up to the sky. They are borne in summer in cool shades of purple, pinkish purple and purple-blue, with bright white centers. Cultivars are available.

E. glomeratus (above & below)

Flowers usually close up at night and on cloudy days.

Features: colorful flowers; spreading habit
Height: 12–18" **Spread:** 24–36"

Celosia
Celosia

C. argentea Plumosa Group (above)
C. argentea Cristata Group (below)

The unusual, wrinkled texture of the celosia's flowers and the incredible variety of flower forms will make any gardener crow with delight.

Growing

Celosia prefers **full sun** and is tolerant of excessive heat. The soil should be **fertile** and **well drained** with **plenty of organic material** worked in. Celosia likes to be watered regularly.

Celosia is a self-cleaning annual, so it does not require deadheading. A plant that has its first flower bloom pinched out will be fuller and bear many more flowers than a plant that has not been pinched.

Tips

Use celosia in borders and beds as well as in planters. The flowers make interesting additions to cut arrangements, either fresh or dried. A mass planting of plume celosia looks bright and cheerful in the garden. The popular crested varieties work well as accents and as cut flowers.

Recommended

C. argentea is the species from which both the crested and plume-type cultivars have been developed. The species itself is never grown. **Cristata Group** (crested celosia) has blooms that resemble brains or rooster combs. This group has many varieties and cultivars in bright, vivid colors. **Plumosa Group** (plume celosia) has feathery, plume-like blooms. This group also has many varieties and cultivars in deep, rich colors.

C. spicata (spiked cockscomb, wheat celosia) produces narrow, spiky flower heads, reminiscent of heads of wheat. Unlike *C. argentea*, spiked cockscombs produce numerous flowers, with an almost shrubby look, in more muted colors. Cultivars are available.

Features: red, orange, gold, yellow, pink or purple flowers **Height:** 10–36"
Spread: 10–36"

Cigar Plant
Cuphea

Cigar plant is definitely a fashion statement and is best used in containers for high traffic areas of the landscape. This plant never fails to generate a plethora of compliments, something that gardeners always appreciate.

Growing

Cigar plant prefers **full sun to partial shade** in **moderately fertile, well-drained soil**. It does best with regular watering but can handle short periods of dryness.

Tips

Cigar plant is an excellent plant for containers of all descriptions. It is also effective in an annual or mixed border and as edging.

Recommended

C. hyssopifolia (Mexican heather, false heather, elfin herb) is a bushy, much-branched plant that forms a flat-topped mound 12–24" tall and slightly wider than the height. The flowers have green calyces and light purple, pink or, sometimes, white petals.

C. ignea (*C. platycentra*; cigar flower, firecracker plant) is a spreading, freely branching plant 12–24" tall and 12–36" wide. The common names relate to the thin, tubular, bright red-orange flowers.

C. llavea (bat-face cuphea, St. Peter plant, tiny mice) is a mounding to spreading plant 12–18" tall and 12–24" wide.

C. ignea (above), *C. llavea* (below)

It produces an abundance of flowers with green to violet calyces and bright red petals. The two longest stamens are bearded purple, giving the flower the appearance of the face of a bat or mouse.

This wonderful plant attracts hummingbirds and butterflies to your garden.

Also called: cigar flower
Features: unique and colorful flowers; habit
Height: 6–24" **Spread:** 10–36"

Cleome
Cleome

C. hassleriana (above & below)

Create a bold and exotic display in your garden with these lovely and unusual flowers.

Growing

Cleomes prefer **full sun** but tolerate partial shade. Plants adapt to most soils, though **mixing in organic matter** to help retain water is a good idea. These plants are drought tolerant but perform best when watered regularly. Pinch out the tip of the center stem on young plants to encourage branching and more blooms. Deadhead to prolong blooming and to reduce prolific self-seeding.

Tips

Cleomes can be planted in groups at the back of a border or in the center of an island bed. These striking plants also make an attractive addition to a large, mixed container planting.

Recommended

C. hassleriana is a tall, upright plant with strong, supple, thorny stems. The foliage and flowers of this plant have a strong but not unpleasant scent. Flowers are borne in loose, rounded clusters at the ends of the leafy stems. Many cultivars are available.

Cleome attracts hummingbirds and provides them with nectar well into fall, because the flowers keep on blooming after many other plants have finished for the year.

Also called: spider flower **Features:** attractive, scented foliage; colorful flowers; thorny stems **Height:** 1–5' **Spread:** 1–2'

Coleus

Solenostemon (Coleus)

There is a coleus for every-one. With foliage from brash yellows, oranges and reds to deep maroon and rose selec-tions, coleus has colors, textures and variations that are almost limitless.

Growing

Coleus prefers to grow in **light** or **partial shade,** but it tolerates full shade if the shade isn't too dense or full sun if the plants are watered regularly. Many new sun-tolerant varieties, which are vegetatively propagated, are available. The soil should be of **rich to average fertility, humus rich, moist** and **well drained**.

Place the seeds in a refrigerator for one or two days before plant-ing them on the soil surface; the cold temperature assists in breaking the seeds' dormancy. The seeds also need light to ger-minate. Seedlings are green at first, but leaf variegation develops as the plants mature.

Tips

The bold, colorful foliage makes a dramatic impact when the plants are grouped together as edging plants or in beds, borders or mixed containers. Coleus can also be grown indoors as a houseplant in a bright room.

When flower buds develop, it is best to pinch them off, because the plants tend to stretch out and become less attractive after they flower.

Features: brightly colored foliage; light purple, insignificant flowers **Height:** 6–36"
Spread: usually equal to height

S. *scutellarioides* mixed cultivars (above & below)

Recommended

S. scutellarioides (*Coleus blumei* var. *verschaffeltii*) forms a bushy mound of foliage. The leaf edges range from slightly toothed to very ruffled. The leaves are usually multi-colored with shades ranging from pale greenish yellow to deep purple-black. Dozens of cultivars are available but many cannot be started from seed.

Cup Flower
Nierembergia

N. hippomanica var. *violacea* 'Mont Blanc' (above), *N. frutescens* 'Purple Robe' (below)

This plant's flowers float like stars atop fern-like foliage. Cup flower is an excellent choice for planting under roses and other complimentary flowering shrubs.

Growing

Cup flower grows well in **full sun** or **partial shade**. It does best in the cooler part of the garden where there is protection from the afternoon sun. The soil should be of **average fertility**, **moist** and **well drained**.

Cup flower is a perennial grown as an annual. During a mild year, it may survive winter. It is often easier to start new plants each year than to over-winter mature plants.

Tips

Use cup flower as a groundcover, for edging beds and borders and for rock gardens, rock walls, containers and hanging baskets. It grows best when summers are cool, and it can withstand a light frost.

Recommended

N. frutescens 'Purple Robe' is a dense, compact plant that produces deep purple flowers with golden eyes.

N. hippomanica var. *violacea* (*N. caerulea*) forms a small mound of foliage. This plant bears delicate, cup-shaped, lavender blue flowers with yellow centers. 'Mont Blanc' is an All-America Selections winner that bears white flowers with yellow centers.

The species name hippomanica *is from the Greek and means 'drive horses crazy.' Whether this means that the horses were 'crazy about' the plant or that they reacted badly to ingesting the plant is unclear.*

Features: blue, purple or white flowers with yellow centers; habit; foliage
Height: 6–12" **Spread:** 6–12"

Euphorbia

Euphorbia

These mounding plants are admired for the bright white bracts that surround their tiny flowers. A second show of color appears in fall when the leaves turn purple, red or orange.

Growing

Euphorbia grows well in **full sun** or **light shade,** in **moist, well-drained, humus-rich soil** of **average fertility**. This plant is drought tolerant and can be invasive in fertile soil. It does not tolerate wet conditions. Plant it in spring or fall.

Propagate euphorbia with stem cuttings. Dip the cut ends in hot water to stop the sticky white sap from running.

Division is rarely required. This plant dislikes being disturbed once established.

Tips

Use euphorbia in a mixed or herbaceous border, rock garden or lightly shaded woodland garden.

Recommended

E. DIAMOND FROST is a Proven Winners, award-winning annual that produces airy, white flowers in great abundance, slightly obscuring the delicate, dark green foliage. It grows 12–18" tall and 10–12" wide.

E. marginata, a native annual, is a vigorous-growing, bushy plant that has bright green, oval leaves with clear white margins. Petal-like white bracts surround tiny clusters of flowers in summer. **'Summer Icicle'** is a dwarf selection with variegated foliage.

E. marginata (above & below)

You may wish to wear gloves when handling this plant, because the sap contains latex, which can irritate the skin.

Also called: ghostweed
Features: colorful bracts; low maintenance
Height: 12–24" **Spread:** 10–12"

Fan Flower
Scaevola

S. aemula (above & below)

Given the right conditions, this Australian plant will flower abundantly from April through to frost.

Fan flower's intriguing, one-sided flowers add interest to hanging baskets, planters and window boxes.

Growing
Fan flower grows well in **full sun** or **light shade**. The soil should be of **average fertility, moist** and **very well drained**. Water regularly because this plant doesn't like to dry out completely. It does, however, recover quickly from wilting when watered.

Tips
Fan flower is popular for hanging baskets and containers, but it can also be used along the tops of rock walls and in rock gardens where it will trail down. This plant makes an interesting addition to mixed borders, or it can be used under shrubs, where the long, trailing stems form an attractive groundcover.

Recommended
S. aemula forms a mound of foliage from which trailing stems emerge. The fan-shaped flowers come in shades of purple, usually with white bases. The species is rarely grown because there are many improved cultivars.

Features: unique blue or purple flowers; trailing habit **Height:** up to 8"
Spread: 36" or more

Firebush
Hamelia

H. patens (above & below)

Firebush is not only an attractive shrub, donning fiery-colored fall foliage and summer flowers, but it is also highly sought after by butterflies, hummingbirds and a variety of other pollinating, nectar-loving insects and birds.

Growing

Firebush prefers **full sun to partial shade**. Any soil will suffice as long as it is **well drained**.

Although this plant is a shrub, it is often grown as a tender perennial or annual throughout Oklahoma.

Also called: scarlet bush, Mexican fire bush
Features: fiery, May to November flowers; colorful fall foliage; habit **Height:** 2–3'
Spread: 1–2'

Tips

Firebush is an ideal specimen plant but also mixes well with other native or non-native shrubs and trees in mixed beds and borders.

Recommended

H. patens is a tropical evergreen shrub that produces softly hairy foliage and an abundance of tubular, mostly red or reddish orange flowers with darker stripes. Later in the season, fruit follows the flowers, changing from green to red to purplish-black. In fall, the foliage changes from the dark green displayed all summer to a variety of reddish shades. Cultivars are available.

Birds are fond of this shrub because of its fruit.

Floss Flower

Ageratum

A. houstonianum 'Hawaii Blue' (above), *A. houstonianum* (below)

The fluffy flowers, often in shades of blue, add softness and texture to the garden.

Growing

Floss flower prefers **full sun** but tolerates partial shade. The soil should be **fertile, moist** and **well drained**. A moisture-retaining mulch prevents the soil from drying out excessively. Deadhead to prolong blooming and to keep plants looking tidy.

The genus name, Ageratum, *is from the Greek, meaning 'without age,' and refers to the long-lasting flowers.*

Tips

The smaller selections, which become almost completely covered in flowers, make excellent edging plants for flower-beds and are attractive when grouped in masses or grown in planters. The taller selections can be included in the center of a flowerbed and are useful as cut flowers.

Recommended

A. houstonianum forms a large, leggy mound that can grow up to 24" tall, though many cultivars have been developed that have a low, bushy habit and generally grow about 12" tall. Flowers are produced in shades of blue, purple, pink or white.

Also called: ageratum **Features:** cool-colored, fuzzy flowers; mounded habit **Height:** 6–36" **Spread:** 6–18"

Gaillardia
Gaillardia

This native annual is sure to turn up the heat in your garden in fiery shades of yellow, red, orange and every shade and combination between. It is the state wildflower of Oklahoma.

Growing

Gaillardia prefers **full sun**. The soil should be of **poor** or **average fertility, light, sandy** and **well drained**. The less water this plant receives, once it is established, the better it does. Don't cover the seeds, because they need light to germinate. They also require warm soil.

Deadhead to encourage more blooms.

Tips

Gaillardia has an informal, sprawling habit that makes it a perfect addition to a casual cottage garden or mixed border. Because it is drought tolerant, it is well suited to exposed, sunny slopes, where it can help retain soil while more permanent plants grow in.

Make sure to place gaillardia in a location where it does not get watered with other plants.

Recommended

G. pulchella forms a basal rosette of leaves. The daisy-like flowers are red with yellow tips. Many cultivars and hybrids exist, including **'Arizona Sun,'** a 2005 All-America Selections winner, bearing fiery-colored flowers earlier than most other cultivars; **'Sundance Bicolor'** bears double flowers in a combination of red, yellow and orange, and **'Torch Yellow'** bears bright yellow blossoms.

Also called: blanket flower **Features:** red, orange or yellow, long-lasting flowers; habit **Height:** 12–36" **Spread:** 12–24"

G. pulchella 'Sundance Bicolor' (above)

Perennial gaillardias are often grown as annuals because of their prolific blooming habit.

Globe Amaranth
Gomphrena

G. globosa (above & below)

Globe amaranth flowers are popular for cutting and drying. Harvest the blooms when they become round and plump; dry them upside down in a cool, dry location.

The flowerheads of globe amaranth are made up of brightly colored, papery bracts from which the tiny flowers emerge.

Growing
Globe amaranth prefers **full sun**. The soil should be of **average fertility** and **well drained**. This plant is drought and heat tolerant and should only be watered during periods of extended drought. Soak seeds in water for two to four days to encourage sprouting before sowing into warm soil above 70° F.

Tips
Globe amaranth can be included in informal and cottage gardens as well as mixed beds and borders. Sometimes overlooked by gardeners because it doesn't start flowering until mid-summer, globe amaranth is worth including in the garden for the long-lasting color it provides from mid-summer to the first frost.

Recommended
G. globosa forms a rounded, bushy plant that grows 12–24" tall. It bears papery, clover-like flowers in shades of purple, magenta, white or pink. Many cultivars are available, including more compact selections like the **Gnome Series**. **'Lavender Lady'** is a taller variety, growing to approximately 16–18" in height.

Features: purple, orange, magenta, pink, white or, sometimes, red flowers
Height: 6–30" **Spread:** 6–15"

Impatiens
Impatiens

I. walleriana (above), *I. walleriana* double-flowered cultivar (below)

Impatiens are the high-wattage darlings of the shade garden, delivering masses of flowers in a wide variety of colors.

Growing

Impatiens do best in **partial** or **light shade** but tolerate full shade. The soil should be **fertile, humus rich, moist** and **well drained**.

Tips

Impatiens are known for their ability to grow and flower profusely, even in shade. Mass plant them in beds under trees, along shady fences or walls or in porch planters. They also look lovely in hanging baskets.

Recommended

I. walleriana (impatiens, busy Lizzie) flowers in shades of purple, red, burgundy, pink, yellow, salmon, orange, apricot or white and can be bicolored. Dozens of cultivars are available.

New impatiens varieties are introduced every year, expanding the selection of sizes, forms and colors for our gardens.

Features: flowers in shades of purple, red, burgundy, pink, yellow, salmon, orange, apricot, white or bicolored; flowers well in shade
Height: 6–36" **Spread:** 12–24"

Lantana
Lantana

L. camara 'Spreading Sunset' (above & below)

Growing

Lantana grows best in **full sun** but tolerates partial shade. The soil should be **fertile, moist** and **well drained**. Plants are heat and drought tolerant. Cuttings can be taken in late summer and grown indoors over winter so you will have plants the following summer.

Tips

Lantana is a tender shrub that is often used as an annual. It grows quickly and makes a stunning addition to mixed planters, combining well with geraniums and other heat-tolerant annuals. It is also an excellent butterfly plant.

Recommended

L. camara is a bushy plant that bears round clusters of flowers in a variety of colors. The flowers often change color as they mature, giving flower clusters a striking, multi-colored appearance. A wide variety of cultivars are available in fiery shades combined with contrasting shades, and creamy white.

L. montevidensis (weeping lantana) is a spreading shrub that produces a dense mat of coarsely toothed foliage. This species bears long-stalked flower stems supporting purple-pink to purple flowers with yellow eyes. It grows 8–36" tall and 24–48" wide.

This low-maintenance plant, with its stunning flowers, thrives in hot weather and won't suffer if you forget to water it.

Also called: shrub verbena **Features:** stunning flowers in shades of yellow, orange, pink, purple, red or white, often in combination **Height:** 8–36" **Spread:** up to 4'

Madagascar Periwinkle

Catharanthus

*M*adagascar periwinkle is a forgiving annual, tolerant of dry spells, searing sun and city pollution. It exhibits grace under all sorts of pressure.

Growing

Madagascar periwinkle prefers **full sun** but tolerates partial shade. Any **well-drained soil** is fine. This plant tolerates pollution and drought but prefers to be watered regularly. It doesn't like to be too wet or too cold. Avoid planting this annual until the soil has warmed because it may fail to thrive if planted in cold or wet soil.

Tips

Madagascar periwinkle does well in the sunniest, warmest part of the garden. Plant it in a bed along an exposed driveway or against the south-facing wall of the house. It can also be used in hanging baskets, in containers and as a temporary groundcover.

C. roseus (above & below)

If this annual is planted in the same spot year after year, a soil-borne pathogen called phytophora may become a problem—switch locations or grow the plant in containers if this occurs.

Recommended

C. roseus (*Vinca rosea*) forms a mound of strong stems. The flowers are pink, red or white, often with contrasting centers.

Many cultivars are available including the '**Jaio Dark Red**,' an All-American Selection from 2003 that produces deep scarlet red flowers with a white eye.

One of the best annuals to use in front of homes on busy streets, Madagascar periwinkle blooms happily despite exposure to exhaust fumes and dust.

Also called: flowering periwinkle
Features: attractive foliage; flowers in shades of red, rose, pink, mauve or white, often with contrasting centers; durability
Height: 6–24" **Spread:** usually equal to or greater than height

Mexican Bush Zinnia

Zinnia

Z. angustifolia 'Classic' (above), *Z. angustifolia* cultivar (below)

Mexican bush zinnias are popular in gardens, adding much-needed color to the late-summer and fall garden.

Growing

Mexican bush zinnias grow best in **full sun**. The soil should be **fertile, rich in organic matter, moist** and **well drained**. To avoid disturbing the roots when transplanting seedlings, start seeds in individual peat pots. Deadhead to prolong blooming and to keep plants looking neat.

Tips

Mexican bush zinnias are useful in beds, borders and containers. The dwarf selections can be used as edging plants. These plants provide wonderful fall color.

Recommended

Z. angustifolia is a low, mounding, mildew-resistant plant that bears yellow, orange or white flowers. It grows to about 8–16" tall. Cultivars are available in bright, vivid colors and a range of sizes.

Mildew can be a problem for zinnias, so choose mildew-resistant cultivars and grow them in locations with good air circulation.

Features: bushy plants; flowers in shades of red, orange, yellow, pink, white or bicolored
Height: 8–16" **Spread:** 12"

Pansy
Viola

V. x wittrockiana (above), *V. tricolor* (below)

Pansies are among the most popular annuals available, and for good reason. They are planted in early fall, often blooming off and on throughout the winter months and are known to put on quite the show in spring. Late-blooming forms can also be planted in late winter.

Growing
Pansies prefer **full sun** but tolerate partial shade. The soil should be **fertile**, **moist** and **well drained**. Pansies do best in cool weather, so plant them in late September through October. It is the heat of summer that kills them, so planting in the spring doesn't give you much time to enjoy them.

Tips
Pansies can be used in beds and borders for winter color or mixed with spring-flowering bulbs. They can also be grown in containers. With the varied color combinations available, pansies complement almost every other type of bedding plant.

Features: blue, purple, red, orange, yellow, pink, white or multi-colored flowers
Height: 3–10" **Spread:** 6–12"

Recommended
V. tricolor (Johnny jump up) is a perennial grown as an annual but will reseed. It bears flowers in shades of purple, lavender blue, white or yellow, with dark purple upper petals. The lower petals are usually streaked with dark purple. Many cultivars exist with larger flowers in various colors above heart-shaped leaves.

V. x wittrockiana is available in a wide variety of hybrids and cultivars that have solid, patterned, bicolored and multi-colored flowers in every size imaginable with face-like markings. The foliage is bright green and lightly scalloped along the edges.

Because of the long growing season, pansies must be occasionally fertilized through winter.

Pentas

Pentas

P. lanceolata 'New Look Red' (above)
P. lanceolata (below)

This plant is a welcome addition to the annual garden, not only for its pretty flowers, but also because it prefers not to be watered too often—ideal for gardeners who aren't very diligent about watering.

Growing

Pentas grows best in **full sun**. The soil should be **fertile**, **moist** and **well drained**. Deadhead to encourage continuous flowering and to keep plants looking tidy. Pinch plants to encourage bushy growth.

Tips

Pentas makes a lovely addition to mixed or herbaceous beds and borders. The coarse, dark foliage creates a background against which brightly colored flowers stand out. It can also be grown in containers, and cuttings taken in late summer can be grown indoors over winter. Pentas is a tremendous butterfly and hummingbird plant.

Recommended

P. lanceolata is a subshrub that is grown as an annual. It has an erect or occasionally prostrate habit. Red, pink, purple or white flowers are produced in clusters. Cultivars are available, including the **New Look Series**.

This plant is often available in the winter to be grown as a houseplant.

Also called: star clusters, Egyptian star
Features: pink, red, purple or white flowers; foliage **Height:** 24–36" **Spread:** 24–36"

Persian Shield
Strobilanthes

This plant's iridescent foliage in metallic shades of purple, bronze, silver and pink adds a bright touch to any annual planting.

Growing
Persian shield grows well in **partial shade**, especially in morning sun with afternoon shade. It can be grown in full sun but wilts in the hottest part of the day even with adequate moisture. The soil should be **average to fertile, light** and **very well drained**. Pinch the growing tips to encourage bushy growth. Cuttings can be started in late summer and overwintered indoors.

Tips
The colorful foliage provides a dramatic background in annual or mixed beds and borders and in container plantings. For stunning contrast, combine Persian shield with plants that have yellow, white, red or purple flowers.

Recommended
S. dyerianus forms a mound of silver- or purple-flushed foliage with contrasting dark green, bronze or purple veins and margins.

S. dyerianus (above & below)

This plant is actually a tender shrub that is treated as an annual. It can be overwintered in a cool, bright location indoors.

Features: decorative foliage and blue flowers
Height: 18–36" **Spread:** 24–36" or more

Petunia

Petunia

P. 'Purple Wave' (above), P. multiflora type (below)

For their speedy growth, prolific blooming, ease of care and huge variety of selections, petunias are hard to beat.

Growing

Petunias prefer **full sun**. The soil should be of **average to rich fertility, light, sandy** and **well drained**. Pinch halfway back in mid-summer to keep plants bushy and to encourage new growth and flowers.

Tips

Use petunias in beds, borders, containers and hanging baskets.

Recommended

P. x *hybrida* is a large group of popular, sun-loving annuals that fall into three categories: **grandifloras** have the largest flowers in the widest range of colors, but they can be damaged by rain; **multifloras** bear more flowers that are smaller and less easily damaged by heavy rain; and **millifloras** have the smallest flowers in the narrowest range of colors, but this type is the most prolific and least likely to be damaged by heavy rain. Cultivars of all types are available and new selections are made available almost every year.

The rekindling of interest in petunias was largely owing to the development of exciting, new selections, such as the Supertunia hybrids and Wave family of petunias. These hybrid series are continuous-blooming, vigorous-spreading, dense-growing, wet-weather-tolerant plants that offer tremendous options for hanging baskets, containers and borders.

Features: colorful flowers; versatile plants
Height: 6–18" **Spread:** 12–24" or wider

Phlox
Phlox

Grow annual phlox and you'll soon find spots for it everywhere, because this showy, easy-to-grow bedding staple adapts to a wide variety of uses.

Growing
Phlox prefers **full sun**. The soil should be **fertile, moist** and **well drained**. This plant is easily grown from seed. Plants can be spaced quite closely together. Deadhead to promote blooming.

Take care when transplanting phlox into the garden, because the roots may resent being disturbed. Seed into peat pots or pellets or into large cell-packs. Do not butterfly the roots when planting.

Tips
Use phlox on rock walls and in beds, borders, containers and rock gardens.

Recommended
P. drummondii forms a bushy plant 6–18" tall and 10" or more in spread. It can be upright or spreading, and it bears clusters of white, purple, pink or red flowers. **Fordhook Finest Mix** is available in shades of dark pink, lavender, white, pale yellow and bicolored. **Twinkle Mixed** includes compact plants 8" tall, with unusual, small, star-shaped flowers. The colors of the petal margins and centers often contrast with the main petal color.

P. drummondii cultivar (above & below)

Start phlox seed again in mid-summer to enjoy late-summer and fall blooms.

Features: colorful flowers; form; drought tolerance **Height:** 6–18"
Spread: 8–10" or more

Pincushion Flower

Scabiosa

S. atropurpurea (above & below)

The rather rag-tag appearance of pincushion flowers brings comfortable charm to the cottage garden and other loose, informal environments.

Growing

Pincushion flowers grow best in **full sun**. The soil should be of **average to rich fertility, alkaline, well drained** and **rich in organic matter**. Keep the soil moderately moist, but do not overwater.

The rounded, densely petaled blooms serve as a perfect landing pad for butterflies.

Tips

Pincushion flowers are useful in beds, borders and mixed containers. The flowers are also popular in fresh arrangements.

Recommended

S. atropurpurea is an upright, branching plant growing up to 36" tall and spreading about 12". The species has purple or crimson flowers; cultivars are available in white or blue. **'Ace of Spades'** has deep maroon flowers with a honey scent; it grows to 24" tall. **'Imperial Giants'** bears blooms in a deep maroon as well as shades of pink.

Features: unique purple, blue, maroon, pink, white, red or bronze flowers; form; habit
Height: 24–36" **Spread:** up to 12"

Rose Moss
Portulaca

For a brilliant show in the hottest, driest, most neglected area of the garden, you can't go wrong with moss rose.

Growing

Moss rose requires **full sun**. The soil should be of **poor fertility, sandy** and **well drained**. To ensure that you will have plants where you want them, start seed indoors. If you sow directly outdoors, the tiny seeds may get washed away by rain and the plants will pop up in unexpected places. Moss rose also self-seeds, and it can provide a colorful show from year to year.

Tips

Moss rose grows well under the eaves of a house or in a dry, rocky, exposed area. It also makes a great addition to a hanging basket on a sunny front porch. Remember to water it occasionally. As long as the location is sunny, this plant does well with minimal care.

Recommended

P. x *grandiflora* (moss rose) forms a bushy mound of succulent foliage. It bears delicate, papery, rose-like flowers profusely all summer. Many cultivars are available, including those with flowers that stay open on cloudy days. **Sundial Hybrids** are particularly popular throughout the state.

P. x grandiflora (above & below)

P. oleracea (ornamental purslane) produces succulent foliage, wider than that of *P.* x *grandiflora,* and single or double, neon yellow flowers. **Yubi Series** is a popular choice with a collection of colors, including apricot, red and pink.

Features: colorful, drought-resistant summer flowers in shades of red, pink, yellow, white, purple, orange and peach **Height:** 4–8"
Spread: 6–12" or wider

Salvia

Salvia

S. *splendens* (above), S. *farinacea* 'Victoria' (below)

With over 900 species of Salvia, you're sure to find one you'll like for your garden.

Salvias should be part of every annual garden—the attractive and varied forms have something to offer every style of garden.

Growing

All salvia plants prefer **full sun** but tolerate light shade. The soil should be **moist, well drained** and of **average to rich fertility,** with a lot of **organic matter.**

Tips

Salvias look excellent grouped in beds and borders and in containers. The flowers are long lasting and make good cut flowers for arrangements.

To keep plants producing flowers, water often and fertilize monthly.

Recommended

S. coccinea (Texas sage) is a bushy, upright plant that bears whorled spikes of white, pink, blue or purple flowers.

S. farinacea (mealy cup sage, blue sage) has bright blue flowers clustered along stems powdered with silver. Cultivars are available.

S. splendens (salvia, scarlet sage) is grown for its spikes of bright red, tubular flowers. Recently, cultivars have become available with flowers in white, pink, purple or orange.

Also called: sage **Features:** colorful summer flowers; attractive foliage
Height: 16–30" **Spread:** 9–14"

Tropical Butterfly Weed

Asclepias

A. curassavica (above & below)

Tropical butterfly weed, a Central and South American native, will attract butterflies to your garden. It is a major food source for the monarch butterfly.

Growing

Tropical butterfly weed prefers **full sun** and **well-drained soil**. It tolerates drought once established but enjoys some moisture in an extended drought. The deep taproot makes division very difficult. To propagate, use the seedlings that sprout up around the base of the plant.

Be careful not to pick off or destroy the green-and-black-striped caterpillars that feed on butterfly weed—they will become beautiful monarch butterflies.

Deadhead to encourage a second blooming.

Tips

Use tropical butterfly weed in meadow plantings and borders, on dry banks, in neglected areas and in wildflower, cottage and butterfly gardens.

Recommended

A. curassavica is an evergreen subshrub that is grown as an annual. It bears red or orange-red flowers, sometimes yellow or white, with tinges of yellowy orange. The foliage is proportionate to the size of the flower clusters and is smooth in texture.

Also called: tropical milkweed, blood flower, Indian root, swallow-wort **Features:** orange, yellow, red or white flowers; attractive form **Height:** 36" **Spread:** 24"

Yellow Bells

Tecoma

T. stans (above & below)

It's difficult not to be impressed by this prolific bloomer. It blooms almost all season long, producing bright, sunny yellow flowers that emit a sweet scent. Yellow bells is useful for a wide variety of gardening applications.

Growing

Yellow bells thrives in **full sun**. Partial shade is tolerated in sandy sites in limestone conditions. **Fertile, moist** but **well-drained soil** with added **organic matter** is best. Regardless of its drought tolerance, yellow bells benefits from supplemental watering during long, dry spells, or flowering will come to a halt.

Tips

Yellow bells can be used in mixed beds and borders as a background plant. This annual is especially stunning when planted with other fiery-blooming plants or those with cool-colored flowers and foliage, including lantana, sun-loving coleus varieties, tropical butterfly weed and goldenrod.

Recommended

T. stans (*Bignonia stans, Stenolobium stans*) is an open shrub or small tree that is often grown as an annual. This species produces bright green foliage and funnel-shaped, lemon yellow, pendulous flowers that can reach 4" in length. The leaves, made up of 5–13 lance-shaped leaflets, are also quite large, reaching 14" in length. The flowers emerge in late winter and continue to be produced until summer. **'Gold Star'** is slightly smaller compared to the species and blooms much earlier and heavier.

Also called: esperanza **Features:** bright yellow flowers; decorative foliage; habit **Height:** 3–4' **Spread:** 3–4'

Artemisia
Artemisia

Most artemisias are valued for their silvery foliage, not their flowers. Silver is the ultimate blending color because it enhances every other hue combined with it.

Growing

Artemisias grow best in **full sun**. The soil should be of **low to average fertility** and **well drained**. These plants dislike wet, humid conditions.

When artemisias begin to look straggly, cut them back hard to encourage new growth and maintain a neater form. Divide them every year or two, when plant clumps appear to be thinning in the centers.

Tips

Use artemisias in rock gardens and borders. Their silvery gray foliage makes them good backdrop plants to use behind brightly colored flowers. They are also useful for filling in spaces between other plants. Smaller forms may be used to create knot gardens. Some artemisias can spread and become invasive in the garden.

Recommended

*A. **ludoviciana*** (white sage, silver sage) is an upright, clump-forming plant with silvery white foliage. The species is not grown as often as its cultivars. (Zones 4–8)

*A. x **'Powis Castle'*** is a compact, mounding, shrubby plant with feathery, silvery gray foliage. This hybrid is reliably hardy to zone 6, but it can also grow in colder

A. stelleriana 'Silver Brocade' (above)
A. ludoviciana 'Valerie Finnis' (below)

regions if planted with winter protection in a sheltered site.

*A. **stelleriana*** has deeply lobed, silvery leaves covered in felt-like hairs. The species can grow 12–18" tall and wide. The cultivars are the most sought-after selections pertaining to this species, and they're available in great abundance, offering decorative foliage and varied sizes and forms.

Also called: wormwood, sage
Features: silvery gray, feathery or deeply lobed foliage **Height:** 6"–4' **Spread:** 12–36"
Hardiness: zones 3–8

Baptisia

Baptisia

B. sphaerocarpa (above), B. australis (below)

Spikes of bright blue flowers in early summer and attractive green foliage make this native plant a worthy addition to any garden, even if it does take up a sizeable amount of garden real estate.

Once established, this tough perennial is unfazed by drought and heat. It resents disturbance, so it doesn't need dividing.

Growing

Baptisia prefers **full sun** but tolerates partial shade, though too much shade causes lank growth that flops over easily. The soil should be of **poor to average fertility, sandy** and **well drained**.

Tips

Baptisia can be used in an informal border or a cottage garden. It is an attractive addition for a naturalized planting, on a slope or in any sunny, well-drained spot in the garden.

Recommended

*B. **alba*** (white wild indigo) is an erect perennial with a bushy growth habit. It bears tall spikes of white flowers that are sometimes marked with purple. It grows 2–4' tall and 2' wide.

*B. **australis*** (false blue indigo) is an upright or somewhat spreading, clump-forming plant that bears spikes of purple-blue flowers in early summer.

B. **'Carolina Moonlight'** grows 4–4^1/$_2$' tall and 3–4' wide. Clusters of soft yellow flowers are borne in late spring. The foliage turns to silvery blue during the hottest period of summer.

B. **'Purple Smoke'** grows 4^1/$_2$' tall, bearing violet flowers with dark purple centers.

*B. **sphaerocarpa*** (yellow wild indigo) grows 2–3' tall and bears yellow flowers in early summer.

Also called: false indigo **Features:** late-spring or early-summer, purple, blue, yellow or white flowers; habit; foliage **Height:** 2–5' **Spread:** 2–4' **Hardiness:** zones 3–9

Black-Eyed Susan

Rudbeckia

R. fulgida var. *sullivantii* 'Goldsturm' (above & below)

The cultivar 'Goldsturm' is an excellent anchor perennial because of its long life, bright yellow flowers and long blooming season. It doesn't need division, won't die out in the center and won't encroach on its neighbors.

Growing

Black-eyed Susan grows well in **full sun** or **partial shade**. The soil should be of **average fertility** and **well drained**. Several *Rudbeckia* species are touted as 'claybusters' because they tolerate fairly heavy clay soils. Established plants are drought tolerant, but regular watering is best. Divide if you wish in spring or fall, every three to five years.

Tips

Black-eyed Susan is a tough, long-lived, low-maintenance perennial. Plant it wherever you want a casual look.

It looks great planted in drifts. Include this native plant in wildflower and natural gardens, beds and borders.

Pinching the plants in June results in shorter, bushier stands.

Recommended

R. fulgida is an upright, spreading plant bearing orange-yellow flowers with brown centers. **Var.** *sullivantii* '**Goldsturm**' bears large, bright, golden yellow flowers.

R. maxima is an upright native perennial with spoon-shaped, large, blue-green foliage and daisy-like, bright yellow flowers with very prominent conical centers that face upward. This species grows 5–6' tall and 2' wide.

Features: bright yellow, orange or red, midsummer to fall flowers with brown or green centers; attractive foliage; easy to grow
Height: 2–6' **Spread:** 1–2'
Hardiness: zones 3–9

Blazing Star
Liatris

L. spicata 'Kobold' (above), L. spicata (below)

Growing

Blazing star prefers **full sun**. The soil should be of **average fertility** and **sandy**. Water well during the growing season but don't allow the plants to stand in water during cool weather. Mulch during summer to prevent moisture loss.

Trim off the spent flower spikes to promote a longer blooming period and to keep blazing star looking tidy.

Tips

Use blazing star in borders and meadow plantings. Plant it in a location that has good drainage to avoid root rot in winter. Blazing star also grows well in planters.

Recommended

L. aspera (rough gayfeather) is a clump-forming, native perennial with densely clustered foliage and purple-spiked flowerheads. This species grows up to 6' tall and 1–2' wide. (Zones 4–9)

L. elegans (pinkscale gayfeather) produces similar flowers to other species but with pale white inner petals. This species grows 2–4' tall and is native to Oklahoma. (Zones 7–9)

L. punctata (snakeroot) is a tuberous native perennial with narrow leaves and dense, purple flowerheads. It grows up to 3' tall and 2' wide. (Zones 3–7)

L. spicata (blazing star, spiked gayfeather) is a clump-forming, erect plant. The flowers are pinkish purple or white. Several cultivars are available.

lazing star is an outstanding cut flower with fuzzy, spiked blossoms above grass-like foliage. It is also an excellent plant for attracting butterflies to the garden.

Features: summer flowers; grass-like foliage
Height: 18"–6' **Spread:** 12–24"
Hardiness: zones 3–9

Blue Star
Amsonia

A. hubrectii (above & below)

Perennials are not known for spectacular fall color, but the species *A. hubrectii* breaks the mold with its spectacular display of stunning, golden yellow fall hues.

Growing

Blue star grows well in **full sun, partial shade** or **light shade**. The soil should be of **average fertility, moist** and **well drained**. This plant is drought tolerant once established. Divide in spring to propagate more plants.

Tips

This pretty plant has a fine, billowy appearance. To achieve the most stunning results, plant it in groups of three to five.

Recommended

A. hubrectii (blue star) forms a clump of arching stems and narrow, bright green leaves. Clusters of small, light blue, star-shaped flowers are produced from late spring to mid-summer. These blooms are followed by stunning, golden yellow fall color.

A. tabernaemontana (willow blue star) is a clump-forming, multi-stemmed perennial that produces dark green foliage and dense, rounded panicles of pale blue flowers. The species grows up to 2' tall and wide. Cultivars and varieties are available with deeper-colored blue and purple flowers.

Features: spring through summer flowers; habit; foliage **Height:** 24–36" **Spread:** 24–36" **Hardiness:** zones 4–9

Cardinal Flower
Lobelia

L. cardinalis (above & below)

These lovely members of the bellflower family contain deadly alkaloids and have poisoned people who tried to use them in herbal medicines.

The brilliant red of these native flowers is motivation enough for some gardeners to install a pond or bog garden, just to meet cardinal flower's moist soil requirements.

Growing

Cardinal flowers grow well in **full sun, light shade** or **partial shade**. The soil should be **fertile, slightly acidic** and **moist**. Avoid letting the soil dry out completely, especially in a sunny location. Mulch plants lightly in winter for protection. Deadhead to keep the plants neat and to encourage a possible second flush of blooms. Plants tend to self-seed, but seedlings may not be identical to parent plants. Seedlings can be moved to new locations or they can be left where they are to replace the short-lived parent plants.

Tips

These plants are best suited to streamside or pondside plantings or in bog gardens. They can also be included in moist beds and borders or in any location where they will be watered regularly.

Recommended

L. cardinalis forms an upright clump of bronze-green leaves and bears spikes of bright red flowers from summer to fall. There are also many hybrids and cultivars available, often with flowers in shades of blue, purple, red or pink. Some hybrids and cultivars are as hardy as the species while others are less hardy.

Features: bright red, purple, blue and pink summer flowers; bronze-green foliage
Height: 24–48" **Spread:** 12–24"
Hardiness: zones 4–9

Catmint

Nepeta

Catmint is an easy-to-grow perennial that provides a wonderful show of flowers all summer long.

Growing

Catmints grow well in **full sun** or **partial shade**. The soil should be of **average fertility** and **well drained**. Plants tend to flop over in soil that is too fertile. Pinch plants back in early June to encourage bushy, compact growth. Cut back after blooming to encourage a second flush of flowers.

Tips

The lower-growing catmints can be used to edge borders and pathways and can also be used in rock gardens. Taller selections make lovely additions to perennial beds. All catmints work well in herb gardens and with roses in cottage gardens.

Recommended

N. **'Blue Beauty'** ('Souvenir d' André Chaudron') forms an upright, spreading clump. It grows 18–36" tall and spreads about 18". The gray-green foliage is fragrant, and the large flowers are dark purple-blue.

N. 'Six Hills Giant' (above), *N.* x *faassenii* (below)

N. x *faassenii* forms a clump of upright, spreading stems. Spikes of blue or lavender flowers are produced in spring and summer and sometimes again in fall. Many cultivars and hybrids are available.

If you grow catmint, you may find that cats are drawn to your garden— this plant is related to catnip (N. cataria), which is well known for its attractiveness to cats.

N. **'Six Hills Giant'** is a large, vigorous plant about 3' tall and about 24" in spread. It bears large, showy spikes of deep lavender blue flowers.

Features: spring or summer flowers; habit; fragrant foliage **Height:** 10–36"
Spread: 18–36" **Hardiness:** zones 3–8

Celandine Poppy

Stylophorum

S. diphyllum (above & below)

Celandine poppy is a low-maintenance, tough-as-nails plant that is native to the eastern U.S. It combines well with other spring-flowering woodland beauties, such as Virginia bluebells.

Growing

This plant grows well in **partial to full shade** in **moist, humus-rich soil** of **moderate fertility**. Keep the plant out of the hot sun, because the foliage can scorch. Plants will go dormant if the soil is allowed to dry out in summer. Divide plants in spring. Celandine poppy does self-seed, and it may become weedy in optimal growing conditions.

Tips

Celandine poppy is a great plant for use in shady woodland gardens and alongside water features. It also looks great at the front of more formal beds and borders. Its tendency to self-seed makes it a great choice for naturalizing.

Recommended

S. diphyllum forms a basal rosette of deeply lobed, mid-green to blue-green foliage that stays attractive after the plant finishes flowering. It bears bright to lemon yellow flowers in abundance in spring and sporadically through summer. The silvery seedpods are covered with hairs.

Do not collect plants or seeds from the wild for this species or for any other plant. Always obtain your plants from reputable sources.

Also called: flaming poppy **Features:** bright yellow spring to summer flowers; attractive foliage; fuzzy seedpods **Height:** 12–18" **Spread:** 12–18" **Hardiness:** zones 4–9

Columbine
Aquilegia

ew flowers signal spring quite so singularly as columbines. Their nodding flowers and spacious foliage look light and graceful wherever you plant them.

Growing

Columbines grow best with **morning sun** and **afternoon shade**. They prefer soil that is **fertile, moist** and **well drained** but adapt well to most soil conditions. Division is not required but can be done to propagate desirable plants. The divided plants may take a while to recover because columbines dislike having their roots disturbed.

Tips

Use columbines in rock gardens, formal or casual borders and naturalized or woodland gardens.

Recommended

A. canadensis (wild columbine, Canada columbine) is a native plant that is common in woodlands and fields. It bears yellow flowers with red spurs.

A. chrysantha var. *hinckleyana* (Hinckley's golden columbine) grows 18–24" tall and 24–36" wide. It bears large, bright yellow flowers and blue-green foliage.

A. x *hybrida* (*A.* x *cultorum;* hybrid columbine) forms mounds of delicate foliage and has exceptional flowers. Many hybrids have been developed with showy flowers in a wide range of colors.

A. canadensis (above)
A. x *hybrida* 'McKana Giants' (below)

A. vulgaris (European columbine, common columbine) has been used to develop many hybrids and cultivars with flowers in a variety of colors.

Columbines self-seed but are not invasive. The new seedlings are often a different color than the parents. Blame it on the bees.

Features: red, yellow, pink, purple, blue or white spring and summer flowers; color of spurs often differs from that of petals; attractive foliage **Height:** 7–30" **Spread:** 12–36" **Hardiness:** zones 3–8

Coneflower

Echinacea

E. purpurea 'Magnus' and 'White Swan' (above), *E. purpurea* (below)

Coneflower attracts wildlife to the garden, providing pollen, nectar and seeds to various hungry visitors.

Coneflower is a visual delight, with its mauve petals offset by a spiky, orange center.

Growing

Coneflower grows well in **full sun** or very **light shade**. It tolerates any well-drained soil but prefers an **average to rich soil**. The thick taproots make this plant drought resistant, but it prefers to have regular water. Divide every four years or so in spring or fall.

Deadhead early in the season to prolong flowering. Later on, you may wish to leave the flowerheads in place to self-seed or to provide winter interest. Pinch plants back or thin out the stems in early summer to encourage bushy growth that are less prone to mildew.

Tips

Use coneflowers in meadow gardens and informal borders, either in groups or as single specimens. The dry flowerheads make an interesting feature in fall and winter gardens.

Recommended

E. purpurea is an upright plant that is covered in prickly hairs. It bears purple flowers with orangy centers. Cultivars are available, including selections with white or pink flowers. Some new hybrids offer an expanded color range of orange or yellow flowers. This species is native to southeastern Oklahoma and is fibrous rooted. All the other species of Echinacea native to our state are taprooted.

Features: mid-summer to fall flowers; persistent seedheads **Height:** 2–5' **Spread:** 12–24" **Hardiness:** zones 3–8

Coral Bells

Heuchera

From soft yellow-greens and oranges to midnight purples and silvery, dappled maroons, coral bells offer a great variety of foliage options for a perennial garden with partial shade.

Growing

Coral bells grow best in **light or partial shade**. The foliage colors can bleach out in full sun, and plants grow leggy in full shade. The soil should be of **average to rich fertility, humus rich, neutral to alkaline, moist** and **well drained. Good air circulation is essential.** Deadhead to prolong the bloom. Every two or three years, coral bells should be dug up to remove the oldest, woodiest roots and stems. Plants may be divided at this time, if desired, then replanted with the crown at or just above soil level.

Tips

Use coral bells as edging plants, in clusters and woodland gardens or as groundcovers in low-traffic areas. Combine different foliage types for an interesting display.

Recommended

There are dozens of beautiful cultivars available with almost limitless variations of foliage markings and colors. See your local garden center or a mail-order catalog to discover what is available.

H. x brizoides 'Firefly' (above)
H. sanguineum (below)

Coral bells have a strange habit of pushing themselves up out of the soil because of their shallow root systems. Mulch in fall if the plants begin heaving from the ground.

Also called: alum root **Features:** very decorative foliage; spring or summer flowers **Height:** 2–4' **Spread:** 6–18" **Hardiness:** zones 3–9

Crocosmia

Crocosmia

C. 'Lucifer' (above), C. 'Norwich Canary' (below)

So that crocosmias' wispy blooms really stand out, use strong backdrop plants such as variegated ornamental grass.

The intense colors of crocosmia are like beacons in the garden.

Growing

Crocosmia prefers **full sun**. The soil should be of **average fertility, humus rich, moist** and **well drained**. This plant needs to be divided every three to five years to keep it vigorous and blooming profusely.

Tips

Crocosmia looks striking when massed in a herbaceous or mixed border. It looks good next to a pond, where the brightly colored flowers can be reflected in the water.

Recommended

C. x *crocosmiiflora* is a spreading plant with long, strap-like leaves and one-sided spikes of red, orange or yellow flowers in mid- and late summer. **'Citronella'** (golden fleece) bears bright yellow flowers.

C. **'Jenny Bloom'** is a vigorous selection with butter yellow flowers on 24–36" tall plants.

C. **'Lucifer'** is the hardiest of the bunch and bears bright scarlet red flowers. Hummingbirds will love you for planting it.

Features: brightly colored flowers in shades of red, orange or yellow; strap-like foliage
Height: 18"–4' **Spread:** 12–18"
Hardiness: zones 5–8

Culver's Root
Veronicastrum

V. virginicum 'Album' (above)

Culver's root provides a strong, vertical accent in beds and borders. Its late-season, pastel blooms are a welcome change from the yellows, oranges and golds that tend to dominate at this time of year.

Growing
Culver's root grows well in **full sun** and **partial shade**. Soil should be **average to fertile, humus-rich** and **moist**. Divide plants in spring or fall when clumps appear to be thinning in the middle or when plants appear to be growing less vigorously.

Tips
The large plants add height to the back and middle of a mixed or herbaceous border. They also make lovely additions to open woodland gardens, meadow plantings and cottage-style gardens, and they work well in the moist soil near a water feature.

Recommended
V. virginicum is an upright perennial that grows 4–6' tall with a spread of 18–36". Spikes of fuzzy-looking white, pink or purple-blue flowers are produced from mid-summer to early fall.
'Album' (var. *album*) bears white flowers.
Var. *incarnatum* ('Roseum') bears pink flowers.
Var. *sibiricum* is a super-hardy variety with long, lavender blue flower spikes.

Also called: Bowman's root Features: white, pink or purple-blue flower spikes from mid-summer to fall; plant form Height: 4–6'
Spread: 18–36" Hardiness: zones 3–8

'Culver' was, supposedly, an early-American physician who used the plant for one or more of its many medicinal applications.

Daylily

Hemerocallis

H. 'Dewey Roquemore' (above), H. 'Bonanza' (below)

The daylily's adaptability and durability combined with its variety in color, blooming period, size and texture explain its popularity.

Growing

Daylily grows in any light from **full sun to full shade**. The deeper the shade, the fewer the flowers will be produced. The soil should be **fertile, moist** and **well drained,** but these plants adapt to most conditions and are hard to kill once established. Divide every two or three years to keep plants vigorous and to propagate them. The plants can, however, be left indefinitely without dividing. Deadhead to prolong the blooming period. Be careful when deadheading purple-flowered daylilies because the sap can stain fingers and clothes.

Tips

Plant daylilies alone, or group them in borders, on banks and in ditches to control erosion. They can be naturalized in woodland or meadow gardens. Small varieties are also nice in planters.

Recommended

Daylilies come in an almost infinite number of forms, sizes and colors in a range of species, cultivars and hybrids. Visit your local garden center or daylily grower to find out what's available and most suitable for your garden.

Features: spring and summer flowers in every color except blue and pure white; grass-like foliage **Height:** 1–4' **Spread:** 1–4' **Hardiness:** zones 2–8

Goldenrod

Solidago

The cultivated varieties of goldenrod tame the unruly appearance of the native species without reducing the profusion of blooms.

Growing

Goldenrod prefers **full sun** but tolerates partial shade. The soil should be of **poor to average fertility, light** and **well drained**. Too fertile a soil results in lush growth, few flowers and invasive behavior.

Divide goldenrod every three to five years in spring or fall to keep it vigorous and to control growth.

Tips

Goldenrod is great for providing late-season color. It looks at home in a large border, cottage-style garden or wildflower garden. Don't plant it near less vigorous plants, because goldenrod can quickly overwhelm them. Goldenrod is a great plant for water-wise gardens.

Recommended

Solidago **hybrids** form a clump of strong stems with narrow leaves. They grow about 2–4' tall and spread about 18–24". Plume-like clusters of yellow flowers are produced from mid-summer to fall. **'Crown of Rays'** holds its flower clusters in horizontal spikes and flowers from mid-summer to fall. **'Fireworks'** has strong, sturdy stems and golden yellow flower spikes that dart horizontally throughout the clump of foliage. **'Golden Shower'** bears flowers in horizontal or drooping plumes.

S. 'Crown of Rays' (above & below)

S. rigida (stiff goldenrod) produces radiant, flat-topped, yellow flowers that grow 3–5' tall.

Goldenrod is not the source of hay-fever pollen; it is ragweed (Ambrosia *species*).

Features: yellow flowers from mid-summer through fall; attractive habit **Height:** 2–5' **Spread:** 18–30" **Hardiness:** zones 3–8

Hardy Hibiscus
Hibiscus

H. moscheutos cultivar (above & below)

It's always hard to convince people that these outsized beauties are really perennials that deserve a place in the garden. Although the extremely large flowers last only a single day, hardy hibiscus stands up to the abuse of an Oklahoma summer.

Growing

Grow hardy hibiscus in **full sun**. The soil should be **humus rich, moist** and **well drained**. Hardy hibiscus is a heavy feeder and benefits from a side dressing of fertilizer when it begins to leaf out. Divide in spring. Prune by one-half in June for bushier, more compact growth. Deadhead to keep the plant tidy. If you cut your hardy hibiscus back in fall, be sure to mark its location because this plant is slow to emerge in spring.

Tips

This plant adds interest to the back of an informal border or in a pondside planting, and it attracts hummingbirds. The large flowers create a bold focal point in late-summer gardens.

Recommended

H. moscheutos is a large, vigorous plant with strong stems. The huge flowers can be up to 12" across. Cultivars are available, including some wonderful plants like **'Cranberry Punch,'** bearing deep reddish pink blossoms.

If a quick freeze follows a wet fall, hardy hibiscus may die out.

Also called: rose mallow **Features:** white, red or pink mid-summer to frost flowers
Height: 18"–8' **Spread:** 36"
Hardiness: zones 4–9

Hens and Chicks
Sempervivum

S. tectorum 'Atropurpureum' and 'Limelight' (above), *S. tectorum* (below)

The genus name *Sempervivum* means 'always living,' which is appropriate for this fascinating and constantly regenerating plant.

Growing

Grow hens and chicks in **full sun** or **partial shade**. The soil should be of **poor to average fertility** and **very well drained**. Add fine gravel or grit to the soil to provide adequate drainage. Once a plant blooms, it dies. When you deadhead the faded flower, pull up the soft parent plant as well to provide space for the new daughter rosettes that sprout up, seemingly by magic. Divide by removing these new rosettes and rooting them.

The little plantlets are simple to pass along. Just separate a 'chick' and you have the start of a whole colony of plants.

Tips

This plant makes an excellent addition to a rock garden or rock wall, where it will grow even right on the rocks. Be careful not to over water this drought-tolerant succulent.

Recommended

S. tectorum is one of the most commonly grown hens and chicks. It forms a low-growing mat of fleshy-leaved rosettes, each about 6–10" across. Small, new rosettes quickly emerge, growing and multiplying to fill almost any space. Flowers may be produced in summer in shades of red, yellow, white and purple but are not as common in colder climates.

Features: succulent foliage; unusual flowers
Height: 3–6"   **Spread:** 12" to indefinite
Hardiness: zones 3–8

Hosta

Hosta

H. sieboldiana 'Elegans' (above)

Breeders are always looking for new variations in hosta foliage. Swirls, stripes, puckers and ribs enhance the leaves' various sizes, shapes and colors.

Growing

Hostas prefer **light** or **partial shade** but will grow in full shade. Morning sun is preferable to afternoon sun in partial shade situations. The soil should ideally be **fertile, moist** and **well drained** but most soils are tolerated. Hostas are fairly drought tolerant, especially if given a mulch to help them retain moisture. Division is not required but can be done every few years in spring or summer to propagate new plants.

Tips

Hostas make wonderful woodland plants and look very attractive when combined with ferns and other fine-textured plants. Hostas are also good plants for a mixed border, particularly when used to hide the ugly, leggy, lower stems and branches of some shrubs. Hostas' dense growth and thick, shade-providing leaves allow them to suppress weeds.

Recommended

Hostas have been subjected to a great deal of crossbreeding and hybridizing, resulting in hundreds of cultivars. Visit your local garden center or get a mail-order catalog to find out what is available. The cultivar **'So Sweet'** is one of the toughest hostas for Oklahoma.

Also called: plantain lily **Features:** decorative foliage; summer and fall flowers **Height:** 4–36" **Spread:** 6"–6' **Hardiness:** zones 3–8

Lamb's Ears

Stachys

S. byzantina 'Big Ears' (above), *S. byzantina* (below)

Named for its soft, fuzzy leaves, lamb's ears has silvery foliage that beautifully contrasts with any bold-colored plants that tower above it, softening hard lines and surfaces.

Growing

Lamb's ears grows best in **full sun**. The soil should be of **poor** or **average fertility** and **well drained**. The leaves can rot in humid weather if the soil is poorly drained. Remove spent flower spikes to keep the plants looking neat.

Tips

Lamb's ears makes a great groundcover in a new garden where the soil has not yet been amended. When used to edge borders and pathways, it provides a soft, silvery backdrop for more vibrant colors next to it. For a silvery accent, plant a small group of lamb's ears in a border.

Recommended

S. byzantina forms a mat of thick, woolly rosettes of leaves. Pinkish purple flowers bloom in early summer. The species can be quite invasive, so choosing a cultivar may be wise. The many cultivars offer a variety of foliage colors, sizes and flowers. **'Big Ears'** ('Countesse Helen von Stein'), is a clump-forming perennial that produces fuzzy leaves twice as large as those of other species or cultivars.

Many plants in the mint family contain antibacterial and antifungal compounds. When lamb's ears is used as a poultice on wounds, it may actually encourage healing.

Also called: lamb's tails, lamb's tongues
Features: soft, fuzzy, silver foliage; pink or purple flowers **Height:** 6–18"
Spread: 18–24" **Hardiness:** zones 3–8

Lanceleaf Coreopsis
Coreopsis

C. lanceolata 'Sunburst' (above), *C. lanceolata* cultivar (below)

This plant produces flowers throughout summer and is easy to grow; it makes a fabulous addition to every garden.

Growing

Lanceleaf coreopsis grows best in **full sun**. The soil should be of **average fertility, sandy, light** and **well drained**. This plant can develop crown rot in moist, cool locations with heavy soil. Too fertile of a soil encourages floppy growth. Deadhead to keep the plant blooming.

Tips

Lanceleaf coreopsis is a versatile plant, useful in formal and informal borders and in meadow plantings and cottage gardens. It looks best when planted in groups.

Recommended

C. lanceolata is a native, clump-forming species with lance-shaped leaves and solitary, yellow flowers. Cultivars are available in dwarf forms and with double flowers.

Mass plant lanceleaf coreopsis to fill in a dry, exposed bank where nothing else will grow, and enjoy the bright, sunny flowers all summer long.

Also called: tickseed **Features:** summer flowers; attractive foliage **Height:** 24" **Spread:** 18" **Hardiness:** zones 4–9

Lenten Rose
Helleborus

H. orientalis cultivar (left & right)

These beautiful, spring-blooming groundcover plants are among the earliest harbingers of spring, providing the welcome sight of what's to come long before most other plants have even started to sprout.

Growing

Lenten roses prefer **light, dappled shade** and a **sheltered location** but tolerate some direct sun if the soil stays evenly moist. The soil should be **fertile, humus rich, neutral to alkaline, moist** and **well drained**. Mulch plants in winter if they are in an exposed location. In a mild winter, the leaves may stay evergreen and flowers may appear as early as February.

Tips

Use these plants in a sheltered border or rock garden, or naturalize them in a woodland garden.

Recommended

H. orientalis (lenten rose) is a clump-forming, evergreen perennial. It grows 12–24" tall, with an equal spread. It bears white or greenish flowers that turn pink as they mature in mid- or late spring.

All parts of lenten rose are toxic, and the leaf edges can be sharp, so wear long sleeves and gloves when planting or dividing these plants.

Also called: Christmas rose **Features:** late winter to mid-spring flowers **Height:** 12–24"
Spread: 12–24" **Hardiness:** zones 4–9

Lungwort
Pulmonaria

P. saccharata (above & below)

The wide array of lungworts have highly attractive foliage that ranges in color from apple green or silver-spotted to olive or dark emerald.

Growing

Lungworts prefer **partial to full shade**. The soil should be **fertile, humus rich, moist** and **well drained**. Rot can occur in very wet soil. Divide in early summer, after flowering or in fall. Provide the newly planted divisions with a lot of water to help them reestablish.

Tips

Lungworts make useful and attractive groundcovers for shady borders, woodland gardens and pond and stream edges.

Recommended

P. saccharata forms a compact clump of large, white-spotted, evergreen leaves and purple, red or white flowers. Many cultivars are available.

To keep lungworts tidy and to show off the fabulous foliage, deadhead the plants by shearing them back lightly after they flower. These plants are unpalatable to deer.

Also called: Bethlehem sage
Features: decorative, mottled foliage; spring flowers **Height:** 12" **Spread:** 24"
Hardiness: zones 4–8

Monkey Grass
Liriope

L. muscari (above), *L. muscari* 'Variegata' (below)

Often confused with mondo grass or *Ophiopogon*, this grass-like perennial is commonly used throughout the state because of its showy flowers, clump-forming growth habit and use as a groundcover and border edging.

Growing

Monkey grass prefers to grow in locations with **full to partial sun**. **Light, moderately fertile soil** that is **moist, slightly acidic** and **well drained** is best.

Tips

Monkey grass is often planted in rows along border edges to create a defined, ornate line that separates the bed from pathways, sidewalks, patios and driveways. Cut the foliage back to within 2–3" from the ground in mid-February so it will be replaced with lush new leaves each spring.

Recommended

*L. **muscari*** is a clump-forming perennial with arching, grass-like foliage. Flower spikes that support bright purple flowers in late summer emerge from the crown. Cultivars are available with white flowers, accompanied by golden variegated, solid and silvery foliage. **'Big Blue'** bears violet-blue flowers, and **'Monroe White'** produces white flower spikes held above dark green foliage. **'Variegata'** produces green leaves with creamy yellow edges and purple flowers. *L. spicata*, another species, runs rampant in the garden.

The flowers are followed by small, black, berry-like fruit.

Also called: lily turf **Features:** purple, violet-blue or white flowers; dense clumps of grass-like foliage **Height:** 12–24" **Spread:** 12–24" **Hardiness:** zones 6–10

Peony
Paeonia

P. *lactiflora* 'Shimmering Velvet' (above)
P. *lactiflora* cultivars (below)

From the simple, single flowers to the extravagant doubles, it's easy to become mesmerized with these voluptuous plants. Once the fleeting, but magnificent, flower display is done, the foliage remains stellar throughout the growing season.

Growing

Peonies prefer **full sun** but tolerate some shade. The planting site should be well prepared before the plants are introduced. Peonies like **fertile, humus-rich, moist, well-drained soil,** to which a lot of compost has been added. Mulch peonies lightly with compost in spring. Too much fertilizer, particularly nitrogen, causes floppy growth and retards blooming. Deadhead to keep plants looking tidy.

Tips

These wonderful plants look great in a border combined with other early bloomers. They can be underplanted with bulbs and other plants that die down by mid-summer; the peonies' emerging foliage will hide the dying foliage of the spring plants. Avoid planting peonies under trees, where they have to compete for moisture and nutrients.

Recommended

There are hundreds of peony species, hybrids and cultivars available. Cultivars come in a wide range of colors, may have single or double flowers and may or may not be fragrant. Visit your local garden center to see what is available.

Place wire peony supports around the plants in early spring to support the heavy flowers. The foliage will grow up and around the wires and hide the grid or wire ring.

Features: spring and early-summer flowers in white, cream, yellow, pink, red or purple; attractive foliage **Height:** 24–32" **Spread:** 24–32" **Hardiness:** zones 2–8

Perennial Salvia
Salvia

S. *greggii* cultivar (above)

Perennial salvias are reliable, hardy members of the perennial border.

Growing

Perennial salvia prefers **full sun** but tolerates light shade. The soil should be of **average fertility, humus rich** and **well drained**. The plants are drought tolerant once established.

Deadhead to prolong blooming. Trim plants back in spring to encourage new growth and to keep them tidy. New shoots sprout from old, woody growth.

Tips

Perennial salvias are attractive plants for the middle or front of the border. They can also be grown in mixed planters.

Recommended

S. *azurea* var. *grandiflora* (azure sage) is an open, upright native plant that produces azure blue blooms in late summer and into fall. (Zones 5–9)

S. *greggii* (autumn sage) is a dwarf, evergreen shrub that is often grown as a woody-based perennial. It branches mainly from the base and produces softly hairy foliage with snapdragon-like, red to purple, yellow or pink flowers from late summer to fall. This species grows 12–24" tall and wide. Cultivars are available with brightly colored, reddish flowers. (Zones 7–9) **'Pink Preference'** is one of the more cold-hardy cultivars of S. *greggii*.

Also called: sage Features: attractive, cream, purple, blue or pink flowers; foliage Height: 1–5' Spread: 1–2' Hardiness: zones 5–9

Russian Sage

Perovskia

P. atriplicifolia (above), *P. atriplicifolia* 'Filigran' (below)

Russian sage offers four-season interest in the garden: soft, gray-green leaves on light gray stems in spring; fuzzy, violet blue flowers in summer; and silvery white stems in fall that last until late winter.

Growing

Russian sage prefers **full sun**. The soil should be **poor to moderately fertile** and **well drained**. Too much water and nitrogen causes this plant's growth to flop, so do not plant it

Russian sage blossoms make a lovely addition to fresh bouquets and dried-flower arrangements.

next to heavy feeders. Russian sage cannot be divided because it is a subshrub that originates from a single stem.

In spring, when new growth appears low on the branches, or in fall, cut the plant back hard to about 6–12" to encourage vigorous, bushy growth.

Tips

The silvery foliage and blue flowers soften the appearance of daylilies and work well with other plants in the back of a mixed border. Russian sage can also create a soft screen in a natural garden or on a dry bank.

Recommended

P. atriplicifolia is a loose, upright plant with silvery white, finely divided foliage. The small, lavender blue flowers are loosely held on silvery, branched stems. Cultivars are available.

Features: mid-summer to fall flowers; attractive habit; fragrant, gray-green foliage **Height:** 3–4' **Spread:** 3–4' **Hardiness:** zones 4–9

Shasta Daisy
Leucanthemum

L. x superbum (above & below)

Shasta daisy is one of the most popular perennials because it is easy to
grow and the blooms are bright, plentiful
and work well as cut flowers.

Growing
Shasta daisy grows well in **full sun** or
partial shade. The soil should be **fertile,
moist** and **well drained**. Pinch or trim
plants back in spring to encourage compact, bushy growth. Divide every year or
two in spring to maintain plant vigor.
Deadheading extends the bloom by several weeks.

Start seeds indoors in spring or direct
sow into warm soil. Fall-planted Shasta
daisy may not become established in
time to survive winter. Plants can be
short-lived in zones 4 and 5.

Tips
Use Shasta daisy as a single plant or
massed in groups. Shorter varieties can
be used in many garden settings, and
taller forms may need support if exposed
to windy situations. The flowers can be
cut for fresh arrangements.

Recommended
L. x superbum forms a large clump of
dark green leaves and stems. It bears
white, daisy flowers with yellow centers
all summer, often until first frost. 'Alaska'
bears large flowers and is hardier than
the species. 'Becky' has strong, wind-
resistant stems, with blooms lasting up
to eight weeks.

Features: white, early-summer to fall flowers
with yellow centers **Height:** 1–4'
Spread: 15–24" **Hardiness:** zones 4–9

Sneezeweed

Helenium

H. autumnale (above & below)

Sneezeweed is one of those 'statement' plants—tall and prairie-esque, with flowers in autumnal shades that start opening in August.

Growing

Sneezeweed grows best in **full sun**. The soil should be **fertile, moist** and **well drained**. When planted in soil that is too rich, it can be short-lived and weak-stemmed. Be sure to water well in summer. Divide every two or three years to keep clumps from becoming overgrown and dying out in the middle. Deadheading helps prolong blooming.

Some support may be needed to hold mature stems upright. Pinch growth back in early summer to encourage lower, bushier growth that is less likely to need support.

Tips

Sneezeweed adds bright color to the border in late summer and fall. It looks at home in informal cottage and meadow gardens. It also works well near a pond or water feature, where it will get regular water.

Recommended

*H. **autumnale*** forms an upright clump of stems and narrow foliage. It grows up to 6' tall and 18–36" wide and bears yellow, red, brown, orange, maroon or bicolored, daisy-like flowers. **'Crimson Beauty'** produces large, crimson-colored flowers and **'Sunball'** ('Kugelsonne') bears lemon yellow and chartreuse flowers. (Zones 3–8)

Helenium is named for Helen of Troy.

Features: colorful, warm flowers; habit
Height: 3–6' **Spread:** 18–36"
Hardiness: zones 3–8

Solomon's Seal
Polygonatum

Solomon's seal is a woodland wildflower with graceful, arching stems that add a horizontal element to an understory planting.

Growing

This perenial prefers **partial to full shade**. Direct afternoon sun can harm or burn this plant. The soil should be **fertile, humus rich, moist** and **well drained**.

Tips

Solomon's seal seems to brighten up the darkest shade garden. It works well in mixed beds and borders but looks most at home in woodland settings or naturalized areas. It is suitable as a groundcover when mass planted.

The berries are highly **poisonous**.

Recommended

P. odoratum grows 24–36" tall and 12–24" wide. It has arching stems and spreads slowly by rhizomes. Pendent, green-tipped, white flowers are borne along the stem in spring to early summer. Black, round berries follow the waxy flowers. **'Variegatum'** has white-edged variegated foliage. New stems are red.

P. odoratum (above & below)

The common name may derive from the scars left on the creeping rhizomes after the flowering stems die off in fall. They were thought to resemble the six-pointed star associated with King Solomon and David.

Also called: fragrant Solomon's seal
Features: foliage; white flowers; habit
Height: 24–36" **Spread:** 12–24"
Hardiness: zones 4–8

Stonecrop
Sedum

S. acre (above), *S.* 'Autumn Joy' (below)

Some 300 to 500 species of *Sedum* are distributed throughout the Northern Hemisphere. Many stonecrop selections are grown for their foliage, which can range in color from steel gray-blue and green to red and burgundy.

Growing

Stonecrops prefer **full sun** but tolerate partial shade. The soil should be of **average fertility, very well drained** and **neutral to alkaline**. Divide in spring when needed.

Tips

Low-growing stonecrops make wonderful groundcovers and additions to rock gardens or rock walls. They also edge beds and borders beautifully. Taller stonecrops give a lovely late-season display in a bed or border.

Recommended

There are many species, hybrids, cultivars and varieties to choose from, ranging from groundcover selections to tall, upright plants. They bloom at different times, but some of the more popular stonecrops are known for their fall blooms. Consult your local garden center for their best recommendations based on your gardening requirements.

Early-summer pruning of upright species and hybrids encourages compact, bushy growth but can delay flowering.

Features: summer to fall flowers; decorative, fleshy foliage **Height:** 2–24" **Spread:** 12–24" or more **Hardiness:** zones 3–8

Toad Lily
Tricyrtis

*T*hese plants, with their peculiar spotted flowers, are sure to draw attention to their shaded corner of the garden.

Growing
Toad lilies grow well in **partial shade, light shade** or **full shade**. The soil should be **fertile, humus rich, moist** and **well drained**. Mulch in winter if snow cover is often inconsistent in your garden.

Tips
These diminutive plants are well suited to plantings in woodland gardens and shaded borders. If you have a shaded rock garden, patio or pond, these plants make good additions to locations where you can get up close to take a good look at the often-spotted flowers.

Recommended
T. hirta forms a clump of light green leaves. It bears white flowers, spotted with purple, in late summer and fall. Many wonderful cultivars are available.

T. hirta cultivar (above), *T. hirta* (below)

If your toad lily fails to bloom before the first frost, you may need to move it to a warmer location in the garden.

Also called: Japanese toad lily
Features: late-summer and fall flowers; attractive foliage **Height:** 24–36"
Spread: 12–24" **Hardiness:** zones 4–9

Yarrow
Achillea

A. *millefolium* 'Paprika' (above)
A. *filipendulina* (below)

Yarrows make excellent groundcovers. They send up shoots and flowers from a low basal point and may be mowed periodically without excessive damage to the plant. Mower blades should be kept at least 4" high.

Yarrows are informal, tough plants with a fantastic color range.

Growing
Grow yarrows in **full sun** in **well-drained soil** of **average fertility**—avoid heavy clay. Yarrows tolerate drought and poor soil and abide, but do not thrive in, heavy, wet soil or very humid conditions. Excessively rich soil or too much nitrogen results in weak, floppy growth. Divide every two or three years in spring to maintain plant vigor. Deadhead to prolong blooming. Once the flowerheads begin to fade, cut them back to the lateral buds. Basal foliage should be left in place over the winter and tidied up in spring.

Tips
Cottage gardens, wildflower gardens and mixed borders are perfect places for these informal plants. They thrive in hot, dry locations where nothing else will grow.

Recommended
Many yarrow species, cultivars and hybrids are available.

*A. **filipendulina*** forms a clump of ferny foliage and bears yellow flowers. It has been used to develop several hybrids and cultivars.

*A. **millefolium*** (common yarrow) forms a clump of soft, finely divided foliage and bears white flowers. Many cultivars exist in a wide range of flower colors.

Features: white, yellow, red, orange, pink or purple mid-summer to early-fall flowers; attractive foliage; spreading habit **Height:** 7"–4'
Spread: 12–36" **Hardiness:** zones 3–9

Arborvitae

Thuja

*A*rborvitaes are found throughout Oklahoma because of their durability, good looks, adaptation to conditions, range of shapes and, perhaps most importantly, soft needles, which are more gentle on bare arms and legs when you're gardening.

Growing

Arborvitae prefers **full sun**. The soil should be of **average fertility, moist** and **well drained**. These plants enjoy humidity and are often found growing near marshy areas. Arborvitae performs best with some **shelter** from wind, especially in winter, when the foliage can easily dry out and give the entire plant a rather brown, drab appearance.

Tips

Large varieties of arborvitae make excellent specimen trees. Smaller cultivars can be used in foundation plantings and shrub borders, and as formal or informal hedges.

Recommended

T. occidentalis (eastern arborvitae, eastern white cedar) is a narrow, pyramidal tree with scale-like needles. Two popular selections are **'Degroot's Spire,'** a slow-growing variety in an upright form, with deep green foliage and a mature size of 6' tall and 2' wide; and **'Golden Globe,'** a rounded, dwarf form with golden yellow foliage. (Zones 2–7; cultivars may be less cold hardy)

T. plicata (western arborvitae, western redcedar) is a fast-growing, narrowly pyramidal tree. It maintains good foliage

T. occidentalis cultivar (above)
T. occidentalis (below)

color all winter. Several cultivars are available including dwarf and variegated varieties. **'Green Giant'** is one of the fastest growing conical selections, growing 3–5' annually, eventually reaching 30–50' heights and 10–20' spreads. (Zones 5–9)

Also called: cedar **Features:** small to large evergreen shrub or tree; foliage; bark; form
Height: 2–60' **Spread:** 2–20'
Hardiness: zones 2–9

Bald-Cypress
Taxodium

T. distichum (above & below)

*People unfamiliar with bald-cypress
usually expect it to be evergreen.
Gasps are often heard when this
deciduous conifer turns color in fall
and defoliates. Plant near water to
double the effect of its fall color.*

Bald-cypress is a tough, dependable tree that can grow well in a variety of conditions and climates.

Growing
Bald-cypress grows well in **full sun,** in **acidic, moist soil,** but it can adapt to most soils and conditions. Highly alkaline soil may cause the foliage to turn yellow (chlorotic), although a particular strain from the Frio River in west Texas performs brilliantly in very alkaline soil and is the best choice for the western part of Oklahoma. Bald-cypress develops a deep taproot but transplants fairly easily when young.

Tips
Bald-cypress can be used as a specimen tree or in a group planting. This fairly large tree looks best with plenty of space around it—it is ideal in a swampy or frequently wet area where few other trees would thrive.

When grown in waterlogged soil or near a water feature, bald-cypress develops gnome-like 'knees,' which are knobby roots that poke up from the water.

Recommended
T. distichum is a slender, conical tree that may grow over 100' tall in the wild. With maturity, it becomes irregular and more rounded, and the trunk becomes buttressed. In fall, the blue-green foliage turns a rusty orange before falling.

Features: conical, deciduous, coniferous tree; attractive habit, trunk and foliage; cones; fall color **Height:** 50–70' or more **Spread:** 18–30' **Hardiness:** zones 4–9

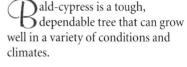

Black Gum
Nyssa

Black gum shines with bright green foliage in summer, giving way to a lovely fall show in shades of yellow, orange, scarlet and purple.

Growing

This tree grows well in **full sun** or **partial shade**. The soil should be **average to fertile, neutral to acidic** and **well drained**. Provide a location with **shelter** from strong winds. Black gum can take a while to get established and dislikes having its roots disturbed, so plant it when it is young and don't attempt to move it again.

Tips

Black gum is a beautiful specimen tree. It can be used as a street tree, but not in polluted situations. Singly or in groups, it is attractive and small enough for a medium-sized property.

Recommended

N. sylvatica (sour gum, black tupelo) is a small to medium-sized, pyramidal to rounded tree. It generally grows 30–50' tall but can reach 100' over time. It spreads about 20–30'. Cultivars offer special characteristics. **'Autumn Cascade'** is a weeping selection. **'Forum'** features a conical form.

Black gum fruit attracts birds but is too sour for human tastes.

N. sylvatica (above), *N. sylvatica* cultivar (below)

Features: pyramidal to rounded, deciduous tree; attractive habit; decorative foliage; fall color **Height:** 10–50' or more **Spread:** 6–30' **Hardiness:** zones 4–9

Boxwood

Buxus

B. *sempervirens* cultivar (above & below)

Growing

Boxwoods prefer **partial shade** but adapt to full shade or to full sun if kept well watered. The soil should be **fertile** and **well drained**. Once established, boxwoods are drought tolerant.

It is best not to disturb the earth around established boxwoods. Using mulch benefits these shallow-rooted shrubs.

Tips

These shrubs make excellent background plants in mixed borders. They are also unattractive to deer so don't suffer from deer browsing.

Recommended

B. microphylla var. *koreana* (Korean littleleaf boxwood) is quite pest resistant and grows about 4' tall, with an equal spread. The bright green foliage may turn bronze, brown or yellow in winter. It is hardy to zone 4. Cultivars are available.

B. sempervirens (common boxwood) can grow up to 20' tall, with an equal spread if it is not pruned. Cultivars are available in varied sizes and forms. **'Suffruticosa'** (edging boxwood) is a compact, slow-growing cultivar that is often used as hedging.

Some of the best boxwood selections are cultivars developed from crosses between the two listed species. These hybrids possess attractive winter color, vigor and a high level of pest resistance common to boxwood. CHICAGOLAND GREEN, **'Green Velvet'** and **'Green Mountain'** are all good selections.

Boxwoods define formality in gardens. These versatile evergreens can be pruned to form neat hedges, geometric shapes or fanciful creatures. When allowed to grow naturally, they form attractive, rounded mounds.

Boxwood foliage contains toxic compounds that when ingested can cause severe digestive upset and possibly death.

Features: dense, rounded, evergreen shrub; foliage; slow, even growth **Height:** 4–20' **Spread:** equal to or slightly greater than height **Hardiness:** zones 4–8

Chaste Tree
Vitex

V. agnus-castus (left & right)

Chaste tree's abundant, long-lasting purple flowers make quite an impression, especially when this shrub is 10–15' tall. Although poorly known in the general gardening population, chaste tree is bound to increase in popularity as more and more people become aware of its merits.

Growing

Chaste tree prefers **full sun** but tolerates partial shade. Any **well-drained, loamy soil** will do.

Chaste tree does not have an extensive root system, so when transplanting, be sure you don't damage the few roots it possesses. The roots should not be exposed to the sun or wind while transplanting in the spring. This shrub can be pruned quite hard, depending on the desired effect and size.

Features: open, rounded habit; aromatic and ornate foliage; purple flowers **Height:** 10–15' **Spread:** 10–15' **Hardiness:** zones 6–9

Tips

This shrub is often integrated into mixed shrub and perennial borders, but it's equally if not more effective when planted as a specimen. Even when not in flower, chaste tree's ornate, scented foliage is striking. If possible, consider planting this shrub close to pathways, windows and patios to please the senses.

Recommended

V. agnus-castus is an open, deciduous shrub with a spreading habit. It bears leaves that emerge from a central stem, similar in appearance to a hand with outstretched fingers. The aromatic foliage is complimented by fragrant, purple flowers borne in upright panicles in early to mid-summer. The flower panicles themselves can grow 12–18" in length.

Chinese Pistache
Pistacia

P. chinensis (above & below)

This tree is the favorite of many gardeners because of its speedy growth habit, fall color and uses in the landscape.

Growing
Grow Chinese pistache in **full sun** in **moderately fertile,** very **well-drained soil.** This tree can tolerate a wide variety of conditions, including drought, pollution, restricted root space and alkaline soil. Younger trees may require staking. Chinese pistache does well when given occasional deep waterings. (Regular shallow watering may induce *Verticillium* wilt.)

Chinese pistache does not respond well to pruning. Train to form when the plants are young. After that, prune minimally, if needed, in late winter.

Tips
Chinese pistache can be used as a street or shade tree. It is effective planted beside patios and does reasonably well in lawns.

Male flowers and female flowers are borne on separate plants. For fruit production, both male and female trees are necessary.

Recommended
P. chinensis has leathery, glossy, dark green foliage that turns a vivid orange to red in fall. The fragrant, inconspicuous flowers bloom in mid- to late spring. Spherical, red fruit follows after the flowers on the female trees.

Features: foliage, flowers, fruit, erect to spreading habit **Height:** 30–60'
Spread: 30–60' **Hardiness:** zones 7–10

Chitalpa

x Chitalpa

*C*hitalpa is the result of crossing *Catalpa bignonioides* and *Chilopsis linearis*. Bringing the best qualities of each genus and species together was not only a good idea but also created a feast for the eyes.

Growing

Chitalpa prefers locations in **full sun** with **well-drained soil**. This vigorous shrub can quickly take over its allotted boundaries and may require a hard pruning in winter and a light pruning during the growing season.

Tips

Chitalpa is well adapted to hot, dry locations as long as the soil drains well.

Recommended

x *C. tashkentensis* is a small- to medium-sized tree with open, upright branches and a rounded form. Its orchid-like, pink blossoms with yellowish centers are produced in July or August at the tips of the branches. Its leaves are longer and broader than *Chilopsis linearis* but much smaller than *Catalpa bignonioides*. This fast-growing, deciduous tree branches readily near its base and grows into a dense, broad form. A few cultivars are available.

x *C. tashkentensis* (above & below)

Chitalpa's drought-resistant nature was inherited from one of the parent plants— the desert willow or Chilopsis linearis.

Features: shrubby, loose and open habit; exotic flowers; lush foliage; drought tolerance
Height: 20–25' **Spread:** 10–15'
Hardiness: zones 6–10

Crapemyrtle
Lagerstroemia

L. indica (above & below)

Crapemyrtle offers a unique element to just about any setting and requires little care for stunning results.

Growing
Crapemyrtle performs best in **full sun** but tolerates light shade. It likes **neutral to slightly acidic, well-drained soil**. In alkaline or salty soil, it may show burnt leaf margins or chlorosis or both. Hot winds may also scorch the leaf margins. Water regularly when young. Plants are drought tolerant but do best with occasional deep watering. Do not water from overhead. This tree may produce suckers and self-seeds readily. Once planted, it does not like to be moved.

Tips
Crapemyrtle is an excellent specimen, large shrub or small tree. Long, cool falls yield the best leaf color.

Crapemyrtle can be trained as a single- or multi-stemmed tree in southern Oklahoma. Elsewhere it will freeze to the ground during really cold winters. Remove lower branches and weak stems to show off the attractive bark.

Remove dead wood in spring. Take care when underplanting around crapemyrtle—the roots are competitive.

Recommended
L. indica bears showy clusters of ruffled, crepe-like flowers in white, red, pink or purple all summer. The bronze-tinged, light green foliage ages to dark, glossy green in summer and turns yellow, orange or red in fall. The gray-brown bark exfoliates to reveal the pinkish bark beneath. Several cultivars are available, but the following selections stand out, namely the **Whit Series** including BURGUNDY COTTON, PINK VELOUR, a 2003 Oklahoma Proven selection, and TIGHTWAD RED, one of the only dwarf crapemyrtles, growing to 2' in height and spread.

Features: upright, deciduous tree or shrub; white, pink, red or purple flowers; attractive foliage; exfoliating bark **Height:** 2–25' **Spread:** 2–25' **Hardiness:** zones 7–10

Dawn Redwood

Metasequoia

Dawn redwood is a refined, pyramidal tree with attractive, deeply furrowed, cinnamon red, flaking bark. Don't worry when this ancient tree drops its needles—it's deciduous.

Growing

Dawn redwood grows well in **full sun** or **light shade**. The soil should be **humus rich, slightly acidic, moist** and **well drained**. Although this tree tolerates wet or dry soils, it prefers humidity and the growth rate is reduced in dry conditions. Provide mulch and water regularly until it is established.

Tips

Dawn redwoods need plenty of room to grow. Large gardens and parks can best accommodate them.

The lower branches must be left in place in order for the trunk to develop its characteristic buttress. Buttressed trunks are flared and grooved, and the branches appear to be growing from deep inside the grooves.

Recommended

M. glyptostroboides has a pyramidal, sometimes spire-like form. The needles turn gold or orange in fall before dropping. The cultivars are narrower than the species. **'Ogon'** has chartreuse foliage during summer.

M. glyptostroboides 'Ogon' (above)
M. glyptostroboides (below)

This tree is often called a 'living fossil' because it was discovered in fossil form before it was found growing in China in the 1940s.

Features: narrow, conical, deciduous conifer; foliage; bark; cones; buttressed trunk
Height: 70–125' **Spread:** 15–25'
Hardiness: zones 5–8

Elm

Ulmus

U. parviflora (above), *U. americana* (below)

The toll taken on elm by Dutch elm disease (DED) is saddening, but certain selections offer a stronger resistance to DED than others, in an attractive, durable package.

Elm seeds are a tasty treat for many small birds. These trees also provide shelter and nesting sites, attracting not only birds but other wildlife as well.

Growing

Elm grows well in **full sun** or **partial shade**. It prefers a **moist, fertile, well-drained soil** but adapts to most soil types and conditions. It tolerates urban conditions, including salt from roadways.

Tips

Often a large tree, elm is attractive where it has plenty of room to grow, such as on large properties and in parks. Small cultivars make attractive specimen and shade trees.

Recommended

There are several elm species and cultivars available, with varied sizes, shapes and appeal, but the following are some of the highly recommended selections based on ease of growth and resistance to DED.

U. alata (winged elm) is a medium-sized tree that grows 30–40' tall with a rounded canopy.

U. americana (American elm) is a vase-shaped tree with pendulous branches and a large, rounded to oval crown. It usually grows 60–80' tall and spreads 30–60', but in the wild it can reach heights well over 100'. The cultivars **'New Harmony'** and **'Valley Forge'** show good DED resistance.

U. crassifolia (cedar elm) is a native, wide-spreading, open tree that grows up to 60' tall.

U. parviflora (Chinese elm, lacebark elm) has a variable growth habit ranging from rounded to upright and vase-like, and it grows 40–50' tall and wide.

Features: attractive rounded to vase-shaped habit; fall color; attractive, mottled bark
Height: 30–80' or more   **Spread:** 30–60'
Hardiness: zones 5–9

False Indigo Bush • Lead Plant

Amorpha

A. fruticosa (left), *A. canescens* (right)

The genus *Amorpha* is native to Oklahoma and typically occurs in open woodlands, glades and prairies. It has made its way into gardeners' hearts, hence its presence in many gardens throughout the state.

Growing

Both species of *Amorpha* prefer to grow in **full sun to partial shade**. The soil should be **well drained, light and sandy**.

Tips

Both lead plant and false indigo bush are often grown for their ability to thrive in poor conditions, including dry and nutrient-deficient soils. Once established, these shrubs can be left to their own devices if low-maintenance plants are what you require in your garden. Mixed borders and beds are an ideal location for this aromatic shrub, especially when planted close in proximity to patios, pathways and decks.

Recommended

A. canescens (lead plant) is a rounded, deciduous shrub that produces small, pea-like, dark purple flowers along a 6" long stem. This species grows up to 3' in height and 5' in spread. The softly hairy leaves are aromatic, deep green in color and decorative in their own right.

A. fruticosa (false indigo bush) is a vigorous, spreading shrub that can grow up to 15' tall and wide. It bears foliage similar to the former species and purple-blue flowers with orange or yellow anthers. The flower spikes are also similar in size to *A. canescens* but are borne shortly before in early summer.

Features: rounded or spreading shrub; ornate flower spikes and foliage **Height:** 3–15' **Spread:** 5–15' **Hardiness:** zones 2–8

Flowering Quince
Chaenomeles

C. speciosa 'Texas Scarlet' (above & below)

One of the loveliest of the later-winter shrubs, quince adds drama and color on even the coldest days.

Beautiful in and out of flower, flowering quince creates an attractive display as a specimen or when trained to grow up or along a brick wall.

Growing
Flowering quince grows well in **full sun**. It tolerates partial shade but produces fewer flowers. The soil should be of **average fertility, moist, slightly acidic** and **well drained**. This shrub is tolerant of pollution and urban conditions.

Tips
Flowering quince can be included in shrub and mixed borders. It is very attractive when grown against a wall, and its spiny habit makes it useful for barriers. Use it along the edge of a woodland or in a naturalistic garden. The dark stem stands out well in winter.

Recommended
C. speciosa (common flowering quince) is a large, tangled, spreading shrub. It grows 6–10' tall and spreads 6–15'. Red, white, pink or coral flowers are borne in late winter, followed by fragrant, greenish yellow fruit. Many cultivars are available, including the popular **'Toyo-Nishiki,'** which produces red, pink and white flowers all on the same plant. **'Cameo'** is a low, compact selection with double, apricot pink blooms. **'Jet Trail'** is also a low grower but has pure white blossoms. **'Texas Scarlet'** produces bright red flowers and is also known for its fruit.

Features: spreading, deciduous shrub with spiny branches; red, pink, white and orange spring flowers; fragrant fruit **Height:** 2–10' **Spread:** 2–15' **Hardiness:** zones 5–8

Ginkgo
Ginkgo

There is not a leaf in the tree kingdom that is as distinctive and elegant as the ginkgo's. Even though a ginkgo tree may not have a perfect crown, just getting close enough to discern the fan-like leaves brings joy to tree lovers.

Growing

Ginkgo prefers **full sun**. The soil should be **fertile, sandy** and **well drained**, but this tree adapts to most conditions. It is also tolerant of urban environments.

Tips

Although its growth is very slow, ginkgo eventually becomes a large tree that is best suited as a specimen tree in parks and large gardens. It can also be used as a street tree. If you buy an unnamed plant, be sure it has been propagated from cuttings. Seed-grown trees may prove to be female, and the stinky fruit is not something you want dropping on your lawn, driveway or sidewalk.

Recommended

G. biloba is variable in habit. The uniquely fan-shaped leaves can turn an attractive shade of yellow in fall. Several cultivars are available.

G. biloba (above & below)

Ginkgo sheds nearly all of its golden fall leaves within a single day, making raking a snap.

Also called: maidenhair tree **Features:** conical in youth, variable with age; deciduous tree; summer and fall foliage; habit; bark; pest free **Height:** 40–100' **Spread:** 10–100' or more **Hardiness:** zones 3–9

Golden Rain Tree

Koelreuteria

K. paniculata (above & below)

Beautiful, tough and adaptable, golden rain tree excels in gardens throughout the state. Few trees share its trait of flowering in summer, and even fewer boast yellow flowers.

Growing

Golden rain tree grows best in **full sun**. The soil should be **average to fertile, moist** and **well drained**. This tree tolerates heat, drought, wind and polluted air. It is also pH adaptable.

Tips

Golden rain tree makes an excellent shade or specimen tree for small properties. Its ability to adapt to a wide range of soils makes it useful in many situations.

The fruit can be messy but does not stain patios or decks. Golden rain tree looks great when underplanted with purple-flowered shrubs, perennials or annuals.

Recommended

K. paniculata is an attractive, rounded, spreading tree that grows 30–40' tall, with an equal or greater width. It bears long clusters of small, yellow flowers. The attractive leaves are somewhat lacy in appearance, and they sometimes turn bright yellow in fall. '**Fastigiata'** is an upright, columnar tree that grows 25' tall and 6' wide. '**Rose Lantern'** produces late summer to early fall flowers in yellow, followed by bluish pink seedpods.

Golden rain tree's unique fruits are conspicuous, lime green, lantern-like capsules that become papery and brown when they mature in late summer to fall.

Features: attractive, rounded, spreading tree; foliage; mid-summer flowers **Height:** 25–40' **Spread:** 6–40' or more **Hardiness:** zones 6–8

Hackberry
Celtis

*H*ackberry tolerates all conditions in Oklahoma, and it responds with brawn and grace.

Growing

Hackberry prefers **full sun**. It adapts to a variety of soil types including poor and dry soils. **Deep soils** with **adequate moisture** and **drainage** are best.

Tips

Hackberry is an ideal shade tree specimen for expansive, windy areas. It grows as tall as it does wide, and it requires lots of space to reach its full size without conflict.

Recommended

C. occidentalis is a medium to large tree with a rounded head. The head is made up of arching branches covered in simple but classic foliage. Inconspicuous flowers emerge in spring followed by dark red or purple, pea-sized fruits in fall.

C. occidentalis (above & below)

Hackberry has everything to offer but asks little in return. It provides magnificent foliar color in fall and cool shade in the hot summer months.

Also called: American hackberry, common hackberry, nettle tree **Features:** rounded, deciduous tree; cold hardiness; colorful berries; tolerance to poor conditions
Height: 30–50' **Spread:** 30–50'
Hardiness: zones 2–8

Holly
Ilex

I. opaca (left), *I. cornuta* cultivar (right)

Hollies are durable shrubs and trees that vary greatly in shape and size. When given conditions they like, they thrive for years.

Growing

These plants prefer **full sun** but tolerate partial shade. The soil should be of **average to high fertility, humus rich** and **moist**. Hollies perform best in **acidic** soil with a **pH of 6.5 or lower. Shelter** hollies from winter wind to help prevent the evergreen leaves from drying out. Apply a summer mulch to keep the roots cool and moist.

Tips

Hollies can be used in groups, in woodland gardens and in shrub and mixed borders. Many can also be shaped into hedges, topiary and espalier with hand pruners.

Recommended

The following holly species do very well in Oklahoma gardens. Many cultivars of different sizes and leaf shapes are available for each of the species. *I. crenata* (Japanese holly), *I. vomitoria* (yaupon) and *I. cornuta* (Chinese holly) are evergreen shrubs. **'Nellie R. Stevens'**, a hybrid of *I. cornuta* and *I. aquifolium*, is a vigorous, conical, evergreen hybrid. It produces the spiny, highly glossy foliage that most gardeners are accustomed to. This hybrid can reach 20' heights and 10' spreads and produces shiny, scarlet fruit. *I. opaca* (American holly) is a large, evergreen tree. *I. decidua* (Possumhaw) is an upright, deciduous shrub with bright green foliage and red or orange fruit. **'Warren's Red'** is more upright and produces bright red fruit and lustrous foliage.

Features: decorative glossy, often spiny foliage; fruit; attractive habit **Height:** 3–20' for shrub species; 40–50' for tree species **Spread:** 3–15' for shrub species; 30–40' for tree species **Hardiness:** zones 3–9

Hoptree

Ptelea

P. trifoliata (left & right)

The name 'hoptree' refers to the resemblance of this tree's fruit to the hops vine fruit. Another much less flattering name for this tree is 'stinking ash,' which relates to the aromatic bark, leaves and flowers. Some people find the scent delightful, while others find it displeasing to the olfactory senses.

Growing

Hoptree prefers locations in **full sun** or with **dappled shade**. The soil should be **fertile** and **well drained**.

Hoptree has several Native American uses as a herbal medicine.

Tips

Hoptree is ideally suited to mixed beds and borders or as a large, flowering specimen.

Recommended

P. trifoliata is an upright, deciduous shrub. It produces aromatic bark, leaves and flowers. The star-shaped flowers are greenish white and are followed by winged, rounded but flattened fruit that is pale green. Cultivars are available including one with bright yellow to green leaves.

Features: upright, deciduous shrub; aromatic flowers, foliage and bark **Height:** 20–25'
Spread: 10–12' **Hardiness:** zones 5–9

Japanese Kerria
Kerria

K. japonica 'Pleniflora' (above & below)

Japanese kerria works very well as a rambling understory shrub in a woodland garden or as a pruned specimen in a shrub border. The bright yellow, spring-blooming flowers, yellow fall foliage and distinctive arching, yellow-green to bright green stems make Japanese kerria an excellent garden addition.

This plant is named for plantsman William Kerr, a fact that aids in the pronunciation of its name.

Growing

Japanese kerria prefers **light, partial** or **full shade,** but it tolerates full sun. The soil should be of **average fertility** and **well drained.** Soil that is too fertile reduces flower production.

Tips

Try using Japanese kerria in group plantings, woodland gardens and shrub or mixed borders.

Recommended

K. japonica grows 3–6' tall and spreads up to 10', bearing yellow single flowers from late winter through early spring. Sporadic flowers may appear in summer. Cultivars are available with variegated foliage, double flowers and pale or white flowers.

Features: upright, arching, dense shrub; late-winter to early-spring flowers in yellow or white
Height: 3–10' **Spread:** 4–10'
Hardiness: zones 4–8

Kentucky Coffee Tree

Gymnocladus

This splendid native is finally receiving the attention it deserves, and it should be given serious consideration when choosing a large shade tree. It matures into an elegant, billowy, feathered cloud of beauty that will be much admired for years to come.

Growing

Kentucky coffee tree grows best in **full sun**. It prefers **fertile, moist, well-drained soil** but adapts to a range of conditions, tolerating alkaline soil, drought and urban situations. Take note, Kentucky coffee tree might not leaf out until late April to early May in the northernmost parts of Oklahoma.

Tips

Ideal for spacious landscapes, parks and golf courses, Kentucky coffee tree makes an attractive specimen tree. It has somewhat brittle branches that may be subject to wind damage.

Recommended

G. dioicus has striking, bluish green foliage with rich yellow fall color and bears large clusters of starry-shaped, greenish white flowers. The ridged bark adds interest to the winter landscape. A variety of cultivars are available.

Kentucky coffee tree rarely suffers from pest or disease problems.

G. dioicus (above & below)

Features: upright to spreading, deciduous tree; summer and fall foliage; fruit; bark
Height: 60–75' **Spread:** 40–50'
Hardiness: zones 3–8

Mahonia
Mahonia

M. bealei (above & below)

Mahonia is a slow-growing, trouble-free shrub that is excellent for attracting birds to your garden. When the blue, grape-like fruits are ripe, the birds devour them with gusto.

The juicy berries are edible but somewhat tart. They can be eaten fresh or used to make jellies, juices or wine—if you get to them before the birds do.

Growing

Mahonia prefers **light** or **partial shade**; full shade may reduce flower production, and full sun is only slightly tolerated, although **protection** from the hot afternoon sun is preferred. The soil should be **neutral to slightly acidic, humus rich, moist** and **well drained**. Provide **shelter** from cold, drying winter winds.

Tips

Mahonia looks great in groups of three or more. Use it in mixed or shrub borders, as a specimen and in woodland gardens. It truly excels as a transition plant between a woodland garden and a more formal garden.

Recommended

M. bealei is an open, upright shrub. Its mildly fragrant, lemon yellow flowers are followed by clusters of light blue berries. The spiny-edged foliage is a dull blue-green and is very leathery.

M. fortunei (Chinese mahonia) is an upright shrub with dark green holly-like foliage and bright yellow flowers. The flowers are followed by round, dark blue berries with a hint of white. This species grows 4' tall and 3' wide.

M. repens (creeping mahonia) is an upright, suckering shrub bearing sharply toothed foliage and dark yellow flowers, which are followed by blue-black berries. A taller cultivar is available.

Features: open, upright shrub; fragrant, yellow late-winter to spring flowers; late-spring to early-summer fruit; leathery foliage **Height:** 1–12'
Spread: 3–10' **Hardiness:** zones 6–9

Maple
Acer

Maples are attractive year-round, with delicate flowers in spring, beautiful foliage and hanging samaras (winged fruit) in summer, vibrant leaf color in fall and interesting bark and branch structures in winter.

Growing
Plant *A. palmatum* in **partial, light** or **full shade,** ensuring shade from the hot afternoon sun and **shelter** from drying winds. Grow *A. rubrum* in **full sun.** The soil should be **fertile,** high in **organic matter, moist** and **well drained.**

Tips
Use maples as specimen, shade or street trees, as large elements in shrub or mixed borders and as hedges. *A. palmatum* is useful as an understory plant bordering wooded areas, and it can be grown in containers on patios or terraces.

Recommended
There are several species and cultivars of maple on the market. The following are some of the more popular selections. Check with your local garden center for their recommendations as well. *A. ginnala* (Amur maple) grows 15–25' tall with an equal or greater spread. It has attractive foliage that turns a brilliant shade of crimson in fall, along with bright red samaras. *A. palmatum* (Japanese maple) generally grows 15–25' tall, with an equal or greater spread, although many cultivars and varieties are much smaller. *A. rubrum* (red maple) is a single- or multi-stemmed tree, growing 40–60' tall, with a variable

A. rubrum (above), A. palmatum cultivar (below)

spread of 20–60'. The fall foliage color varies from bright yellow to orange or red. *A. saccharum* (sugar maple) is one of the most impressive and majestic maples, growing 50–80' tall and 35–50' wide, in a rounded pyramidal form. The **'Caddo'** sugar maple is a name given to a relic population of these trees from Caddo County in western Oklahoma. This population sports a tougher demeanor than other sugar maples and grows to only 30–50' tall. *A. truncatum* (purple-blow maple, Shantung maple) is a compact, rounded tree with lush foliage that turns a bright yellow in fall.

Features: rounded, dense, deciduous tree or shrub; decorative foliage, bark and form; samaras; fall color; greenish flowers
Height: 15–80' **Spread:** 15–60'
Hardiness: zones 4–8

Nandina

Nandina

N. domestica (above & below)

Nandina has so much to offer in the landscape, including glorious foliage and berry color, a tough constitution and an evergreen habit. Few others possess such year-round color and versatility.

Growing

Nandina prefers **full sun** or **partial shade,** in **humus-rich, moist, well-drained soil.** It is prone to chlorosis when planted in alkaline soils. It prefers to be watered regularly but can tolerate drier conditions. Shrubs in full sun that experience some frost produce the best fall and winter color.

The colorful berries of nandina persist through winter and attract birds, which then spread the seeds.

Tips

Use nandina in shrub borders, as a background plant and for informal hedges or screens. It is also a great plant for containers. Mass planting ensures a good quantity of the shiny, bright red berries.

Recommended

N. domestica produces clumps of thin, upright, lightly branched stems and fine, textured foliage. It grows 6–8' tall and spreads 3–5' wide, slowly proliferating by suckering. It bears large, loose clusters of small, white flowers followed by persistent, spherical fruit. Initially tinged bronze to red, the foliage becomes light to medium green in summer, with many varieties turning red to reddish purple in fall and winter. Many colorful, compact and dwarf cultivars are available including **'Firepower,'** a dwarf selection with bright red foliage and **'Nana Purpurea,'** which produces fiery red winter foliage.

Also called: sacred bamboo, common nandina, heavenly bamboo **Features:** white, late-spring to early-summer flowers; fruit; decorative foliage; tough; long-lived **Height:** 18"–8' **Spread:** 18"–5' **Hardiness:** zones 6–9

Oak

Quercus

The oak's classic shape, outstanding fall color, deep roots and long life are some of its many assets. Plant it for its individual beauty and for posterity.

Growing

Most oaks grow well in **full sun,** in **fertile, slightly acidic, moist, well-drained soil**. These trees can be difficult to establish; transplant them only when they are young. Oaks grow fast for their first ten years of life and then slow down.

Tips

Oaks are large trees that are best as specimens or for groves in parks and large gardens. Do not disturb the ground around the base of an oak; these trees are very sensitive to changes in grade.

Recommended

Here are some of the best selections for Oklahoma. **Q. macrocarpa** (bur oak, mossycup oak) is a large, broad tree with furrowed bark, growing 50–80' tall and wide. **Q. rubra** (northern red oak) is a rounded, spreading tree that grows 60–75' tall and wide. Fall color ranges from yellow to red-brown. **Q. shumardii** (Shumard oak, Shumard red oak) is a broad, spreading tree with red fall color. This species grows 40–70' tall and 40–60' wide.

Q. macrocarpa (above)

Oaks belong to one of two groups, the Red Oak Group (Erythrobalanus), or the White Oak Group (Lepidobalanus). Red oaks have leaves that are typically acutely lobed with hair-like awns on the edge and acorns that mature on the previous year's wood. White oaks have leaves that are typically round lobed with no awns and acorns that mature on the current season's wood.

Features: large, rounded, spreading, deciduous tree; summer and fall foliage; attractive bark; acorns **Height:** 40–80' **Spread:** 40–100' **Hardiness:** zones 4–9

Redbud

Cercis

C. canadensis (above & below)

Redbud is not as long lived as many other trees, so use its delicate beauty to supplement more permanent trees.

This outstanding native plant is the official state tree of Oklahoma and is truly a welcome sight in spring. The intense, deep magenta buds open to pink flowers that cover the long, thin branches in clouds of color. Redbud is one of Oklahoma's best understory trees.

Growing

Redbud grows well in **full sun, partial shade** or **light shade;** it appreciates some protection from the hottest afternoon sun. The soil should be a **fertile, deep loam** that is **moist** and **well drained**. This plant has tender roots and does not like being transplanted.

Tips

Redbud can be used as a specimen tree, in a shrub or mixed border and in a woodland garden. A locally grown redbud will perform best in your garden.

Recommended

C. canadensis (eastern redbud) is a spreading, multi-stemmed tree that bears red, purple or pink and occasionally white flowers. The young foliage is bronze, fading to green over summer and turning bright yellow in fall. Many beautiful cultivars and varieties are available including **var.** *texensis* **'Oklahoma,'** which bears waxy but glossy, rich green leaves and dark wine red flowers and was discovered in the Arbuckle Mountains of south-central Oklahoma.

C. chinensis (Chinese redbud) is a densely branched shrub or small tree with leathery, glossy foliage and lavender pink flowers.

Features: spreading, dense tree or shrub; red, purple, pink or white spring flowers; seedpods; fall color **Height:** 15–30' **Spread:** 12–30' **Hardiness:** zones 6–9

Rose-of-Sharon

Hibiscus

H. syriacus cultivar (above), *H. syriacus* 'Red Heart' (below)

*I*f you're aspiring for a tropical look in your backyard, then look no further. Rose-of-Sharon will bring you back to the tropics each summer, and you won't even have to leave home.

Growing

Rose-of-Sharon prefers **full sun** but tolerates partial shade. It responds well in **fertile** soil that is **humus rich, moist** and **well drained**, but it tolerates poor soil and wet spots.

Pinch young shrubs to encourage bushy growth. You can train young plants to form a single-stemmed tree by selectively pruning out all but the strongest stems. The flowers form on the current year's growth; prune back the tip growth in late winter or early spring for larger but fewer flowers.

Tips

Rose-of-Sharon is best used in shrub or mixed borders.

It develops unsightly bare branches toward its base as it matures, so plant low, bushy perennials or evergreen shrubs around the base to hide the bare stems. Rose-of-Sharon can also be grown to form a small tree.

Recommended

H. syriacus is an erect, multi-stemmed shrub that bears dark pink flowers from mid-summer to fall. Many cultivars are available, including **'Blue Bird'** that bears large, blue flowers with red centers and **'Red Heart'** that produces white flowers with dark red centers.

Features: bushy, upright, vase-shaped, deciduous shrub; mid-summer to fall, solid or bicolored flowers **Height:** 8–12'
Spread: 6–8' **Hardiness:** zones 5–10

Smoke Tree
Cotinus

C. coggygria (above & below)

The 'smoke' is all an illusion. Smoke tree produces inconspicuous yellow flowers in early summer. When the flower stalks mature, long, feather-like hairs emerge and change to pink or purple, giving the effect of puffs of smoke.

Growing

Smoke tree grows well in **full sun** or **partial shade**. It prefers soil of **average fertility** that is **moist** and **well drained**. Established plants adapt to dry, sandy soils. Smoke tree is very tolerant of alkaline, gravelly soil.

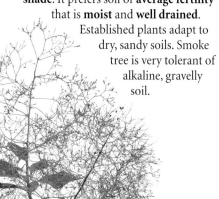

Tips

Smoke tree can be used in a shrub or mixed border, as a single specimen or in groups. It is a good choice for a rocky hillside planting.

Recommended

C. coggygria is a bushy, rounded shrub that develops large, puffy plumes of flowers that start out green and gradually turn a pinky gray. The green foliage turns red, orange and yellow in fall. Many cultivars are available. **'Pink Champagne'** produces pink-beige flowers, **'Royal Purple'** has purplish red flowers and dark purple foliage and **'Velvet Cloak'** bears dark burgundy foliage that turns reddish purple in fall.

Also called: smokebush **Features:** bushy, rounded, spreading, deciduous tree or shrub; early-summer flowers; summer and fall foliage; easy to grow **Height:** 8–15' **Spread:** 8–15' **Hardiness:** zones 4–8

Southern Wax Myrtle
Myrica

Southern wax myrtle is a wonderful native shrub that can stand alone as a specimen or blend easily into a mixed border.

Growing

Southern wax myrtle grows well in **full sun** or **partial shade**. It adapts to most soil conditions, from poor, sandy soil to heavy clay soil. Southern wax myrtle tolerates salty conditions, making it useful where winter road spray may kill less tolerant plants. It rarely needs pruning.

Tips

This adaptable plant forms large colonies and can be used for mass plantings in underused areas. Single plants can be included in borders or used as specimens.

Recommended

M. cerifera (wax myrtle) is a rounded, evergreen shrub. It takes on an upright form, bearing lance-shaped, aromatic foliage and inconspicuous greenish yellow catkins, followed by grayish white fruit that remains on the branches throughout winter. This species grows 15' tall and wide. (Zones 6–9)

M. cerifera (above & below)

These plants fix nitrogen in the soil, much like legumes do, which may explain the ability of southern wax myrtle to perform well in poor soils.

Also called: bayberry **Features:** aromatic, deciduous to semi-evergreen shrub; foliage; dense, suckering habit; persistent fruit
Height: 5–15' **Spread:** 5–15'
Hardiness: zones 3–9

Spirea
Spiraea

S. japonica 'Little Princess' (above), *S.* x *vanhouttei* (below)

Spireas are old-fashioned shrubs that became cutting-edge choices when dwarf, colorful types were introduced. Now that groundcover varieties are available, spireas are approching cutting-edge status again.

Growing
Spireas prefer **full sun**. To help prevent foliage burn, provide **protection** from very hot sun. The soil should be **fertile, acidic, moist** and **well drained**.

Tips
Spireas are popular because they adapt to a variety of situations and require only minimal care once established. They are used in shrub or mixed borders, in rock gardens and as informal screens and hedges.

Recommended
Many species and cultivars are available, including the following very popular selections. **S. japonica** (Japanese spirea) forms a clump of erect stems and bears pink or white flowers. **S. nipponica** is an upright, spreading shrub with arching branches, dark green foliage and cup-shaped, white flowers in mid-summer. **'Snowmound'** is a vigorous, spreading cultivar with a prolific flowering habit. **S. prunifolia** (bridalwreath spirea) is a large, arching shrub with finely toothed leaves and copious amounts of double white flowers in late spring. **S. x vanhouttei** (Vanhoutte spirea) is a dense, bushy shrub with arching branches that bears clusters of white flowers.

Spireas, seen in so many gardens and with dozens of cultivars, remain undeniable favorites.

Features: round, bushy, deciduous shrub; summer flowers; habit **Height:** 2–8' **Spread:** 2–8' **Hardiness:** zones 3–9

Sweet Pepper Shrub

Clethra

C. alnifolia 'Hummingbird' (above), *C. alnifolia* cultivar (below)

Sweet pepper shrub bears wonderfully fragrant flowers in summer. It attracts butterflies and other pollinators and is one of the best shrubs for adding fragrance to your garden.

Growing

Sweet pepper shrub grows best in **light** or **partial shade**. The soil should be **fertile, humus rich, acidic, moist** and **well drained**. This plant tolerates poorly drained, organic soils.

Tips

Although not aggressive, sweet pepper shrub tends to sucker, forming a colony of stems. Use it in a border or in a woodland garden. The light shade along the edge of a woodland is an ideal location.

Try one of the new dwarf cultivars at the front of a border to better enjoy the lovely fragrance.

Recommended

C. alnifolia is a large, rounded, upright, colony-forming shrub with attractive spikes of highly fragrant, white flowers. The foliage turns yellow in fall. '**Anne Bidwell**' produces fragrant, white flowers. '**Hummingbird**' is compact and low growing. '**Ruby Spice**' has deep pink, fade-resistant flowers. WHITE DOVE is a semi-dwarf selection with brilliant white, sweetly scented flowers.

Also called: sweet pepperbush, sweetspire, summersweet clethra **Features:** rounded, suckering, deciduous shrub; fragrant summer flowers; attractive habit; colorful fall foliage
Height: 2–8' **Spread:** 2–8'
Hardiness: zones 3–9

Winter Jasmine

Jasminum

J. nudiflorum (above & below)

Winter jasmine is a great plant for winter interest. The green stems stand out against our gray winter background, and the bright yellow flowers bloom very early in the growing season.

Growing

Winter jasmine grows well in **full sun** or **partial shade,** in **moderate to fertile, well-drained soil.** This drought-tolerant plant adapts to most soil conditions.

Trained as a vine to grow on a trellis, winter jasmine can reach 15' or more in height.

Tips

The long, trailing stems of winter jasmine make an excellent groundcover. Rooting where the stems touch the ground, this tough plant forms large, dense colonies. It is very effective on hard-to-access slopes and in areas with less than ideal soils. Winter jasmine can also be grown in a shrub or mixed border; when it is planted in a container, the stems can dangle over the sides.

Recommended

J. nudiflorum is a spreading, mounding, deciduous plant with slender, arching to trailing, green stems. It grows 3–10' tall and spreads 4–10' wide. In winter and early spring, unscented, yellow flowers appear before the attractive, shiny, dark green foliage emerges. The foliage develops no fall color.

Features: slender, deciduous shrub; dark green foliage; yellow flowers; attractive habit
Height: 3–10' or more **Spread:** 4–10'
Hardiness: zones 6–9

Ballerina

Modern Shrub Rose

This popular hybrid musk rose can produce a plethora of flowers not only in the first flush but in the second as well, rarely leaving you wanting more.

Growing

This rose tolerates light shade but prefers to grow in **full sun**. The soil should be **well drained** and **moderately fertile,** but this rose selection is tolerant of poor soil conditions.

The flowers may need deadheading after the first flush to keep the plant productive.

Tips

With its arching growth habit, Ballerina is suitable for hedging, mixed borders, exhibition, cutting, containers and mass groupings. It can also be trained as a short climber on a trellis or fence.

Recommended

Rosa '**Ballerina**' is a hybrid musk rose that bears large, cascading clusters of single, dainty flowers. The lightly speckled flowers emerge a soft pink with a pale reverse and well-defined pink edges. The pink fades to a pinkish white eye at the base of the petals surrounding the golden stamens. The flowers are supported by a dense mass of small, semi-glossy leaves on almost-thornless stems. Tiny, orange-red hips follow the flowers in fall.

This rose was given its name because the blooms resemble a ballerina's skirt, but the flowers have also been compared to apple blossoms.

Features: mid-season, repeat-blooming, pinkish white, scented flowers; habit **Height:** 4–6'
Spread: 4' **Hardiness:** zones 6–9

Belinda's Dream

Modern Shrub Rose

Belinda's Dream will provide you with successive flushes of fragrant, double, pink blossoms against blue-green, disease-resistant foliage, resulting in a nearly perfect landscape rose.

Growing

Belinda's Dream prefers locations in **full sun,** but it tolerates light shade. The soil should be **well drained** and **moderately fertile**.

Tips

This modern shrub rose works well in mixed borders and is especially effective when planted in large groups, as low hedging or en masse.

Recommended

Rosa **'Belinda's Dream'** is a shrub rose with characteristics of a hybrid tea, such as the high center bloom and long stem. It is a fast-growing shrub with a sturdy, upright habit, and it produces fully double, pink blossoms in repeat flushes.

Dr. Bayse, who developed Belinda's Dream, often breeds roses that are thornless, hardy, drought tolerant and disease resistant. This rose may have never made it to the marketplace because of its thorns, but he finally agreed to release it in 1988 and named it after the daughter of a friend.

Features: fragrant, double, pink flowers; habit **Height:** 4–5' **Spread:** 3–4' **Hardiness:** zones 5–9

Carefree Wonder

Modern Shrub Rose

*T*he name of this shrub rose is perfectly appropriate; this rose requires very little care and produces copious flowers in waves throughout summer.

Growing
Carefree Wonder prefers **full sun** but tolerates some shade. The soil should be **average to fertile, humus rich, slightly acidic, moist** and **well drained**, but this rose has proven to be quite adaptable to a variety of soil conditions. Carefree Wonder is disease resistant. Deadhead to encourage blooming.

Tips
Carefree Wonder makes a great addition to a mixed bed or border, and it is attractive when planted in groups. It can also be mass planted to create a large display, and it is equally attractive as a specimen.

Recommended
Rosa **'Carefree Wonder'** is a bushy, rounded shrub with glossy, dark green, deeply serrated foliage. Clusters of double, pink flowers with silvery undersides to the petals are borne for most of the summer. There are several other roses in the **Carefree Series,** including **'Carefree Beauty'** with medium pink, double flowers and **'Carefree Sunshine'** with yellow flowers.

The color of the flowers varies with the weather and the age of the bloom, ranging through bright to light shades of pink.

Also called: Dynastie **Features:** pink flowers; rounded habit; summer foliage; long blooming period; attractive, orange hips; disease resistant **Height:** 3–5' **Spread:** 3–5' **Hardiness:** zones 4–9

Chuckles

Floribunda Rose

This floribunda rose is a hardy selection that produces deep pink, single flowers with a touch of white in the center. It emits a strong but pretty scent.

Growing

Chuckles thrives in **full sun** but tolerates light shade. **Moderately fertile, well-drained, moist** and **humus-rich soil** is best.

Tips

Chuckles is an outstanding rose for planting in large groups for maximum effect. It also works well along pathways, mixed beds and borders and even in containers.

Recommended

Rosa '**Chuckles**' bears long, pointed, pink buds, which open into flat, semi-double to single blooms reaching 4" in diameter and composed of 11 petals each. The flowers occur in clusters and will repeat bloom at least once throughout the growing season. The pink blossoms contrast nicely against the leathery, dark green leaves.

This floribunda rose was bred by Roy E. Shepherd and released into the marketplace in 1958.

Features: strongly scented, single or semi-double, pink flowers; repeat bloom **Height:** 3–4' **Spread:** 3–4' **Hardiness:** zones 4–9

Dortmund

Modern Shrub Rose • Climbing Rose

*F*ew roses are as respected as much as Dortmund. The foliage alone makes it worth having in the garden.

Growing

Dortmund requires reasonably good growing conditions to thrive. Plant in **full sun** in **fertile, humus-rich, slightly acidic, moist, well-drained soil**. Dortmund tolerates light, dappled shade and poorer soils and is highly disease resistant.

Deadhead heavily and frequently to encourage blooming. Discontinue deadheading at least five weeks before first frost to allow the plant to form a large crop of bright red hips in fall.

Tips

This selection can grow large enough to cover one side of a small building. To create a medium shrub useful for hedging or as a specimen, prune to control the size. As a climber, Dortmund can be trained up a pillar, veranda post, wall or trellis. It can also be grafted as a weeping standard.

Recommended

Rosa 'Dortmund' is a tall, upright plant with dense, glossy, dark green foliage. It bears large, red flowers with a glowing central white eye and bright yellow stamens from spring to fall, with the majority of blooms occurring in spring. It is a little slow to bloom in spring, but once it begins to take off, the results are worth the wait. The flowers have a light apple scent.

Features: attractive foliage; abundant, red flowers with a white eye; growth habit; repeat blooming **Height:** 14–24' **Spread:** 8–10' **Hardiness:** zones 5–9

Graham Thomas

English Rose • Austin Rose

Growing

This rose prefers **full sun to partial shade**. The soil should be **moderately fertile, well drained but moist** and rich with **organic material**.

Deadheading may be required to extend the prolific blooming cycle.

Tips

In our climate, this extremely vigorous rose reaches greater heights when supported, developing into a pillar-style or climbing rose. A light pruning allows Graham Thomas to remain a little smaller, if desired. Its narrow, upright growth habit makes this rose useful as a specimen or toward the back of a mixed border.

Developed in 1983 by David Austin Roses Limited, Graham Thomas was the first true yellow English rose. It was named after one of the most influential rosarians of our time.

Graham Thomas received the Royal Horticultural Society Award of Garden Merit in 1993.

Recommended

Rosa **'Graham Thomas'** bears beautiful, apricot pink buds that open into large, golden yellow blooms. The double blooms carry up to 35 petals and fade gracefully in time. The 4–5" wide flowers remain cupped until the petals fall cleanly from the plant. This rose is very dense and upright in form, bearing an abundance of light green leaves. Long, flexible stems often flop under the weight of the beautiful but short-lived flowers.

Also called: English Yellow, Graham Stuart Thomas **Features:** repeat-blooming, golden yellow flowers **Height:** 3½–7' **Spread:** 4–5' **Hardiness:** zones 6–9

Knockout

Modern Shrub Rose • Landscape Rose

This rose is simply one of the best new shrub roses to hit the market in years. Even people who have never grown roses before are planting this rose in their gardens.

Growing

Knockout grows best in **full sun**. The soil should be **fertile, humus rich, slightly acidic, moist** and **well drained**. This rose blooms most prolifically in warm weather but has deeper red flowers in cooler weather. Deadhead lightly to keep the plant tidy and to encourage prolific blooming.

Tips

This vigorous rose makes a good addition to a mixed bed or border, and it is particularly attractive when planted in groups of three or more. It can be mass planted to create a large display or grown singly as an equally beautiful specimen.

Recommended

Rosa '**Knockout**' has a lovely, rounded form with glossy, green leaves that turn to shades of burgundy in cool weather. The bright, cherry red flowers are borne in clusters of 3–15 almost all summer long and even into fall. Orange-red hips last well into winter. '**Double Knockout**,' '**Pink Knockout**' and a light pink selection called '**Blushing Knockout**' are all available. All varieties have excellent disease resistance.

Features: rounded habit; light, tea rose scented, mid-summer to fall flowers in shades of pink and red; disease resistant **Height:** 3–4' **Spread:** 3–4' **Hardiness:** zones 4–10

Marie Daly

Polyantha Rose

Marie Daly is a new variety of Marie Pavie, an old garden rose which dates back to 1888. Marie Pavie is a superb polyantha rose with white blossoms. The only difference between the two is Marie Daly's distinctly pink color.

Growing

Marie Daly prefers **full sun** and **well-drained soil**, with **adequate organic matter and humus** and **consistent moisture**. Marie Daly is an outstanding performer in almost any soil type, thriving in acidic and even highly alkaline soils.

Tips

Marie Daly is one of the best roses for growing in a large container on a sunny patio or deck. Polyanthas typically produce small flowers in large clusters and are primarily used in containers and for planting en masse or within mixed borders.

Recommended

Rosa 'Marie Daly' has few thorns and produces successive flushes of very fragrant, semi-double to double, pink blooms from spring to frost. It also produces lush, bluish green foliage that is highly resistant to disease and pests.

Marie Daly is considered to be one of the best dwarf landscape roses for Oklahoma gardens.

Features: fragrant, semi-double to double, pink flowers **Height:** 3–4' **Spread:** 3–4' **Hardiness:** zones 5–9

Mister Lincoln

Hybrid Tea Rose

$\mathcal{T}$he blooms of Mister Lincoln are among the darkest red of any red rose. Herbert C. Swim and O.L. Weeks introduced this rose in 1964. It boasts immense, velvety, deep red flowers and a scent reminiscent of damask roses.

Growing

Mister Lincoln prefers locations in **full sun** but can tolerate partial shade. This rose thrives in **hot, dry conditions**. The flowers and foliage don't burn in the hot sun as easily as other red roses do, however the deep red flower color eventually fades to magenta. The soil should be **well drained, rich with organic matter** and **moist**.

Tips

Use Mister Lincoln as a specimen in a garden or at the back of a rose bed or border.

Recommended

Rosa **'Mister Lincoln'** produces urn-shaped buds that open to fully double flowers that first emerge cupped, resulting in a flat, classic high-centered form. Each flower consists of 30–40 petals. The flowers' beauty is enhanced by dark, semi-glossy, leathery foliage.

Mister Lincoln is at its most beautiful when the flowers completely unfurl, exposing the bright yellow stamens.

It has been one of the most popular hybrid tea roses in its color class or category since its release.

Other names: Mr. A. Lincoln, Mr. Lincoln, President Lincoln **Features:** dark red, 4–5½" wide, intensely damask-scented flowers **Height:** 4–5' **Spread:** 30"–3½' **Hardiness:** zones 7–9

Pearly Gates

Climbing Rose

Pearly Gates is a sport of America, a large-flowered climbing rose. Pearly Gates is very similar in appearance and form, but it produces soft, pastel pink blossoms compared to America's deep coral salmon flowers.

Growing

Pearly Gates thrives in **full sun** but tolerates locations in partial shade. The soil should be **moist, well drained** and **organically rich**.

Tips

This climber is ideally suited to climbing up a variety of supports including pergolas, arbors, trellis, obelisks and stair or deck railings. The flowers are perfect for cutting because of their long stems and lasting qualities. Pearly Gates' upright growth habit is also suitable as a pillar-style rose.

Recommended

Rosa '**Pearly Gates**' produces pastel pink, fully double blooms in large clusters. This rose is a repeat bloomer with consistent flushes of flowers. The flowers emit a strong clove spice and old rose scent.

This rose was bred by Lawrence E. Meyer and released into the market in 1999. Soft, pastel pink blossoms are an unusual color for a climbing rose.

Features: 4–5" pastel pink, double flowers; repeat blooming **Height:** 8–12'
Spread: dependent on support
Hardiness: zones 5–9

American Bittersweet

Celastrus

*A*merican bittersweet is a rough-and-tumble, low-maintenance, woody climber that lends a wild look to your garden. Highly decorative clusters of fruit burst forth in fall.

Growing

American bittersweet grows well in **full sun** and tolerates partial shade. It prefers **poor soil** but adapts to almost any soil that is well drained.

Male and female flowers usually bloom on separate plants. Both sexes, planted in close proximity, are needed for fruit production. American bittersweet is often sold with a male and a female plant in one pot. Water them well.

Tips

American bittersweet belongs at the edge of a woodland garden and in a naturalized area. It quickly covers fences, arbors, trellises, posts and walls. As a groundcover, it can mask rubble and tree stumps, and it effectively controls erosion on hard-to-maintain slopes. All parts of American bittersweet are said to be **poisonous**.

This vine can damage or kill young trees or shrubs if allowed to twine around the stems.

Recommended

C. scandens (American bittersweet, staff vine) is a vigorous, twining vine with dark green, glossy foliage that turns bright yellow in fall. Small, yellow-green to whitish flowers bloom in late spring followed by showy fruit. **'Indian Brave'** and **'Indian Maid,'** the male and female cultivar pair, are hardier than the species.

Features: fast growth; twining stems; fruit; fall color **Height:** 6½–10' **Spread:** 3–6' **Hardiness:** zones 3–8

C. scandens (above & below)

Generally, one male plant will pollinate six to nine female plants. The subsequent berry production is very attractive to birds.

Black-Eyed Susan Vine
Thunbergia

Black-eyed Susan vine is a useful, annual-flowering vine with simple flowers dotting the plant, giving it a cheerful, welcoming appearance.

Growing

Black-eyed Susan vine does well in **full sun, partial shade** or **light shade**. Grow it in **fertile, moist, well-drained soil** that is high in **organic matter**.

Tips

Black-eyed Susan vine can be trained to twine up and around fences, walls, trees and shrubs. It is also attractive trailing down from the top of a rock garden or rock wall or growing in mixed containers and hanging baskets.

Recommended

*T. **alata*** is a vigorous, twining climber. It bears yellow flowers, often with dark centers, in summer and fall. Cultivars with large flowers in yellow, orange or white are available.

T. alata (above & below)

Plants grown in containers and hanging baskets can be brought indoors for winter if acclimated to the lower light levels and kept in a bright, cool location.

Features: twining habit; yellow, orange, violet-blue or creamy white, dark-centered flowers
Height: 5' or more   **Spread:** 5' or more
Hardiness: tender perennial treated as an annual

Carolina Jessamine

Gelsemium

Most gardeners are familiar with Carolina Jessamine. It is known to scamper up large trees, fences and even utility poles. Golden yellow flowers adorn this sprawling vine in spring.

Growing

Carolina jessamine thrives in locations with **full sun**. It can grow in partial shade but produces fewer flowers. The soil should be **moist, well drained** and **fertile**.

Pinch the new growth back to encourage a more dense growth habit. Cut it back to approximately 2–3' high when the growth is thin at the bottom and the top is falling over because of the weight. This vine should be pruned only immediately after flowering.

Tips

This vine can be grown on a decorative trellis, a pergola or an arbor. It is often used to adorn mailboxes and just about anything that requires a bit of color and a vertical element.

All parts of this plant are **poisonous**.

Recommended

G. sempervirens is a vigorous vine that produces twining stems without the aid of tendrils. Masses of fragrant, funnel-shaped flowers are borne in late winter, in shades of golden to pale yellow. Dark glossy foliage on rich brown stems is the perfect compliment to the brightly colored blossoms.

G. sempervirens (above & below)

This vine can also be used as an effective groundcover when maintained. For the best results, plant it in a place where it can be allowed to roam and won't be bothered once established.

Features: bright yellow flower clusters; lush foliage; habit **Height:** 15–20' **Spread:** 4–5'
Hardiness: zones 7–9

Cross Vine

Bignonia

B. capreolata 'Jeckyll' (above & below)

Cross vine is sometimes confused with trumpet creeper. Although the two plants look somewhat similar, cross vine doesn't have the same invasive nature, and it blooms at a different time throughout the growing season.

This native vine is known to grow very large and at a rapid rate. It blooms like crazy and disguises unsightly surfaces and structures in no time.

Growing

Cross vine can tolerate a wide range of soil conditions but prefers **organically rich, well-drained** soils in **full sun**. Partial sun is tolerated but the plant may flower less.

Prune after flowering and when you find it necessary to train it on its support.

Tips

This twining plant climbs up just about anything. The stems climb by holdfast disks at the end of their tendrils and rootlets, which act like little suction cups. When first planted, cross vine needs to be attached to the surface it will eventually climb. Any type of garden structure will work, as will stone or brick walls, fences, poles and trees.

Recommended

B. capreolata is a twining, vigorous vine that produces lush, green foliage along long, tough stems. Orange-yellow, tubular flowers with reddish throats emerge in spring and early summer. The foliage takes on a purplish red color as the days grow cooler in winter. Cultivars are available in other fiery colors as well.

Features: bright, fiery-colored flowers; vigorous twining habit **Height:** 30–50' **Spread:** 20–40' **Hardiness:** zones 6–9

Honeysuckle

Lonicera

L. *sempervirens* cultivar (left)
L. *sempervirens* (right)

Honeysuckle vines can be rampant twining vines, but with careful consideration and placement, they won't overrun your garden. The fragrance of the flowers makes any effort worthwhile.

Growing

Honeysuckle grows well in **full sun** or **partial shade**. The soil should be **average to fertile, humus rich, moist** and **well drained**.

Tips

Honeysuckle can be trained to grow up a trellis, fence, arbor or other structure. In a large container near a porch, it will ramble over the edges of the pot and up the porch railings with reckless abandon.

Features: creamy white, yellow, orange, red and scarlet late-spring and early-summer flowers; twining habit; fruit **Height:** 6–12' **Spread:** 6–12' **Hardiness:** zones 4–9

Recommended

There are dozens of honeysuckle species, hybrids and cultivars. Check with your local garden center to see what is available. The following is one of the more popular species.

L. sempervirens (trumpet honeysuckle, coral honeysuckle) bears orange or red flowers in late spring and early summer. Many cultivars and hybrids are available with flowers in yellow, red or scarlet, including the yellow-flowering '**John Clayton.**'

Ipomoea

Ipomoea

I. batatas 'Margarita' (above)

Vines within this group are easy to grow and are bound to make even the beginner feel like an expert.

Growing

Grow ipomoea vine in **full sun**. Any soil will do, but a **light, well-drained** soil of **poor fertility** is preferred.

Soak seeds for 24 hours before sowing. Start seeds in individual peat pots if sowing indoors. Plant in late spring.

Tips

Add sweet potato vine to mixed planters, window boxes and hanging baskets. In a rock garden it scrambles about, and when grown along the top of a retaining wall, it cascades over the edge.

Morning glory and moon vines embellish a wire topiary or any object thin enough to twine around. They grow on fences and walls and up trees, trellises and arbors. Stand back—these vines grow fast. They cover any obstacles they encounter.

Recommended

I. alba (moonflower) has sweet-scented, white flowers that open at night.

I. batatas (sweet potato vine) is a twining climber grown for its attractive foliage. Several cultivars are available.

I. lobata (firecracker vine, spanish flag; syn. *M. lobata*) is a perennial vine often grown as an annual. It bears crimson-flushed stems and stalks clothed in toothed, deeply lobed, green leaves and tubular flowers that emerge in shades of scarlet red but mature to a pale yellow. This species can reach 6–15' heights. Cultivars are available in shades of yellow to cream.

I. nil has bristly stems and white, funnel-shaped flowers with a touch of pale deep blue, purple or red. This vigorous species grows 15' or more in height and spread.

I. tricolor (morning glory) produces purple or blue flowers with white centers. Many cultivars are available.

Features: decorative foliage; fast growth; white, blue, pink or purple and variegated flowers; colorful foliage **Height:** 1–15' **Spread:** 1–15' **Hardiness:** annual

Passion Flower

Passiflora

Passion flower is mesmerizing. It is a fast-growing, woody climber that is grown as an annual in the colder parts of the state. In zone 6 and above, it should thrive for years without any winter protection next to a house. Most passion flower varieties are native to North America.

Growing

Grow passion flower in **full sun** or **partial shade**. This plant prefers **well-drained, moist soil** of **average fertility**. Keep it **sheltered** from wind and cold.

Tips

Passion flower is a popular addition to mixed containers and makes an unusual focal point near a door or other entryway.

Many garden centers sell passion flower in spring. This plant quickly climbs trellises and other supports over summer. It can be composted at the end of summer or cut back and brought inside to enjoy in a bright room over winter.

The foliage tastes like peanut butter, and the small, round fruits are edible but not very tasty.

Recommended

P. incarnata (maypops) is a vigorous, native climbing vine that produces tendrils to attach itself to a support. It has deeply lobed, ornate foliage and bowl-shaped, fragrant, pale purple to nearly white blossoms, with purple and white coronas, which are followed by yellow fruit. This species can reach more than 10' heights.

Features: exotic flowers with white or pale pink petals and blue or purple bands; habit; foliage **Height:** 6' or more **Spread:** variable **Hardiness:** zones 6–10

Fertilize passion flower sparingly. Too much nitrogen encourages lots of foliage but few flowers.

Porcelain Berry
Ampelopsis

A. brevipedunculata (left & right)

This vine has attractive foliage, colorful berries, a reliable and vigorous growth habit and incredible fall color. Finally, a vine that has year-round interest.

Growing

Porcelain berry requires **full to partial sun** in a **moist** but **well-drained location**. Prune after flowering, if flowering on the previous year's growth or from late winter to spring, if flowering on current year's growth.

Porcelain berry is often grown for its attractive foliage, which turns a stunning shade of red and yellow in the cool days of fall.

Tips

Porcelain berry is ideal for climbing up a trellis or support, arbor or pergola. Because of their vigorous growth habit, this vine can cover a wall, fence or old tree in no time at all.

Recommended

A. brevipedunculata is a vigorous climbing vine. The leaves resemble grape leaves and are large in size. Clusters of small green flowers emerge in summer, followed by green berries that change to light blue and finally to purple. **'Elegans'** is a little less vigorous than the species and produces dark green foliage with mottled white and pink markings.

Features: colorful berry clusters, ornate foliage and habit **Height:** 10–15'
Spread: variable **Hardiness:** zones 5–8

Virginia Creeper • Boston Ivy

Parthenocissus

Virginia creeper and Boston ivy are handsome vines that establish quickly and provide an air of age and permanence, even on new structures.

Growing

These vines grow well in any light from **full sun to full shade**. The soil should be **fertile** and **well drained**. The plants adapt to clay or sandy soils.

Tips

Virginia creepers do not require support because they have clinging rootlets that can adhere to just about any surface, even smooth wood, vinyl or metal. Give the plants lots of space and let them cover a wall, fence or arbor. They can also be used as groundcovers.

Recommended

P. quinquefolia (Virginia creeper, woodbine) has dark green foliage. Each leaf, divided into five leaflets, turns flame red in fall.

P. tricuspidata (Boston ivy) produces glossy, dark green foliage reminiscent of grape leaves. The foliage turns shades of orange and red in fall. This self-climber can grow quite tall in a short time.

P. quinquefolia (above & below)

Virginia creeper can cover the sides of buildings, helping to keep rooms cool in the summer heat. Cut the plants back to keep windows and doors accessible.

Features: summer and fall foliage; clinging tendrils **Height:** possibly 30–50', but limited by the size of support **Spread:** same as height **Hardiness:** zones 3–8

Wisteria

Wisteria

W. frutescens 'Amethyst Falls' (left)
W. macrostachya 'Aunt Dee' (right)

Loose clusters of purple hang like lace from the branches of wisteria. With prudent pruning, a gardener can create beautiful tree forms and attractive arbor specimens.

Growing

Wisteria grows well in **full sun** or **partial shade**. The soil should be of **average fertility, moist** and **well drained**. Too fertile a soil produces lots of vegetative growth but very few flowers. Avoid planting wisteria near a lawn where fertilizer may leach over to your vine.

To keep wisteria blooming sporadically all summer, prune off flowering spikes as soon as the flowers fade. A long-handled pole pruner works well. Wisteria will send out new blooming shoots until frost.

Tips

This vine requires something to twine around, such as an arbor or other sturdy structure. Select a permanent site; wisteria doesn't like to be moved. It may send up suckers and can root wherever branches touch the ground. All parts of this plant are **poisonous**.

Recommended

W. frutescens (American wisteria) is a twining climber clothed in divided leaves composed of 9–15 leaflets. Pea-like, fragrant flowers are borne in pendulous, lilac clusters. The flowers are followed by smooth, green seedpods, 4" in length. Cultivars are available with lilac blue or white flowers.

W. macrostachya (Kentucky wisteria) is very similar to the former species in appearance, but the flowers produced by this species are twice as long, reaching 12" lengths.

Features: blue, purple, pink or white flowers; foliage; twining habit **Height:** 20–30'or more
Spread: 20–30' or more
Hardiness: zones 6–9

Arum

Arum

This shade-loving plant will provide you with seasonal interest from early fall through the coldest months of winter and into spring.

Growing

Arum grows well in locations with **partial shade** with shelter from the afternoon sun. The soil should be **humus rich** and **well drained**. Mulch once the leaves have emerged. Divide only when flowering decreases. Large leaves form in a partially shaded location while more sun increases flowering.

Tips

Arum is often planted as an understory plant. It's also useful and quite lovely in shady perennial borders when planted with other ornamental foliage plants that appear to glow in the shade.

Plant the tubers in fall, weeks prior to the first hard frost. They should be planted at least 3" deep and 12" apart.

A. italicum (above), *A. italicum* 'Pictum' (below)

Recommended

A. italicum is a tuberous perennial with spear-shaped, dark to medium green leaves that are veined in white and showy from fall through spring. In spring, pale greenish white flowers, called spathes, emerge. The spathes are followed by bright orange-red berries that last for several weeks. **'Pictum'** produces leaves that are narrower than the species with cream-colored veins.

Arum is the perfect companion plant for hostas, as arum rouses from its summer sleep when the hostas are going dormant.

Features: ornate foliage; white spathes; orange-red fruit **Height:** 12–20" **Spread:** 12–24" **Hardiness:** zones 6–9

Caladium

Caladium

C. *bicolor* cultivar (above)
C. *bicolor* 'Sweetheart' (below)

Caladium's midribs and veining on the striking foliage only strengthen the color combinations, helping draw the eye to its smashing leaf display. If you are searching for bold texture in the garden, this group of plants is a must.

Growing

Caladium prefers to grow in **partial to full shade** although a few sun-tolerant selections are available. They like **moist, well-drained, humus-rich, slightly acidic soil.**

Caladiums are tuberous plants that can be grown from seed but are best grown from tubers. Make sure the knobby side of the tuber is facing up and is level with, or just under, the soil surface. Start growing tubers inside in soil-less planting mix with a minimum soil temperature of 70° F. Once they have leafed-out, the tubers can handle cooler soil temperatures (minimum 55° F).

Dig tubers in fall after the leaves die back. Remove as much soil as possible and let them dry for a few days. Store them in slightly damp peat moss at 55–60° F. Divide tubers in spring before planting. Divisions are subject to fungal diseases because of the freshly exposed surfaces.

Tips

Caladiums provide a tropical feel to your garden. They do very well around water features and in woodland gardens. They are equally effective in herbaceous borders en masse or as specimens and are wonderful plants for containers. When grown in containers there is no need to dig the tubers in fall. Simply bring the whole container inside for the winter.

All parts of caladium may irritate the skin, and ingesting this plant causes stomach upset.

Recommended

C. bicolor (*C.* x *hortulanum*) is native to the edge of woodlands in South America. The often-tufted, arrow-shaped foliage is dark green and is variously patterned with red, white, pink, green, rose, salmon, silver and bronze. Each leaf is 6–12" long.

Also called: elephant's ears, heart-of-Jesus, mother-in-law plant, angel wings
Features: ornate, patterned and colorful foliage; habit; form Height: 18–24" Spread: 18–24"
Hardiness: treat as an annual

Cannas

Canna

Cannas are stunning, dramatically large foliage plants that give an exotic flair to any garden.

Growing

Cannas grow best in **full sun** in a **sheltered** location. The soil should be **fertile, moist** and **well drained**. Plant out in spring after the chance of frost has passed and once the soil has warmed. Plants can be started early indoors in containers to get a head start on the growing season. Deadhead to prolong blooming.

Tips

Cannas can be grown in a bed or border. They make dramatic specimen plants and can even be included in large planters.

Recommended

A wide range of cannas is available, including cultivars and hybrids with green, bronzy, purple or yellow-and-green-striped foliage. Dwarf cultivars that only grow 18–28" tall are also available.

Cannas are cold hardy up through zone 7; in other zones, the rhizomes can be lifted after the foliage is killed back in fall. Clean off any clinging dirt and store the rhizomes in a cool, frost-free location in slightly moist peat moss. Check on them regularly during winter and if they start to sprout, pot them and move them to a bright window until they can be moved outdoors.

C. hybrid (above & below)

Features: decorative foliage; white, red, orange, pink, yellow and bicolored summer flowers Height: 3–6' Spread: 20–36" Hardiness: zones 7–9; the rhizomes over-winter most years throughout Oklahoma if heavily mulched.

Chinese Ground Orchid

Bletilla

B. striata (above & below)

Chinese ground orchid is one of the wonderful surprises that you may encounter in flower this spring.

Growing

Chinese ground orchid grows well in **sheltered** locations with **partial shade**. The soil should be **moist,** very **well drained** and **humus rich**. Mulch around the base to conserve moisture.

Tips

Woodland gardens are the perfect setting for Chinese ground orchid. Because this plant requires shelter and shade, plantings under pergolas and understories are ideal to ensure it is protected from any environmental extremes. It can also be used for naturalizing under the canopy of trees.

Recommended

B. striata is a terrestrial orchid that bears long, wide, blade-like leaves from the base that emerge from a flattened pseudobulb. Pendulous, magenta flowers poke through the strap-like foliage on wiry stems. Selections with white, cream and pale yellow flowers are also available.

This is a species of terrestrial orchid originating from southern Japan and China. In Japan the species is called shi-ran, meaning 'purple orchid.' In China it's known as pai chi.

Features: pink, white, cream or pale yellow, spring to early-summer flowers; rich foliage
Height: 12–24" **Spread:** 12–24"
Hardiness: zones 5–8

Crocus

Crocus

C. x *vernus* cultivars (above & below)

Crocuses are harbingers of spring. They often appear, as if by magic, in full bloom from beneath the melting snow.

Growing

Crocuses grow well in **full sun** or **light, dappled shade**. The soil should be of **poor to average fertility** and **well drained**. The corms should be planted about 4" deep in fall.

Tips

Crocuses are almost always planted in groups. Drifts of crocuses can be planted in lawns to provide interest and color while the grass still lies dormant. They can be left to naturalize in beds or borders. Groups of plants will fill in and spread out to provide a bright welcome in spring.

Recommended

Many crocus species, hybrids and cultivars are available. The spring-flowering crocus most people are familiar with is **C.** x ***vernus***, commonly called Dutch crocus. Many cultivars are available with flowers in shades of purple, yellow and white, sometimes bicolored or with darker veins.

Saffron is obtained from the dried, crushed stigmas of C. sativus. *Six plants produce enough spice for one recipe. This fall-blooming plant is hardy to zone 6 and can be grown successfully in the mildest parts of Oklahoma.*

Features: purple, yellow, white or bicolored, early-spring flowers **Height:** 2–6"
Spread: 2–4" **Hardiness:** zones 3–8

Daffodil

Narcissus

Many gardeners automatically think of large, yellow, trumpet-shaped flowers when they think of daffodils, but there is a lot of variety in color, form and size among the daffodils.

Growing

Daffodils grow best in **full sun** or **light, dappled shade**. The soil should be **average to fertile** and **well drained**. Bulbs should be planted in fall, 2–8" deep, depending on the size of the bulb. The bigger the bulb, the deeper it should be planted. A good general rule to know how deeply to plant is to measure the bulb from top to bottom and multiply that number by three.

Tips

Daffodils are often planted where they can be left to naturalize, in the light shade beneath a tree or in a woodland garden. In mixed beds and borders, the summer foliage of other plants hides the faded daffodil leaves. Do not cut or mow the leaves until they turn yellow.

Recommended

Many species, hybrids and cultivars of daffodils are available. Flowers range from $1^{1}/_{2}$–6" across and can be solitary or borne in clusters. There are 13 divisions of daffodils based on flower form and heritage categories.

The cup in the center of a daffodil is called the corona, and the group of petals that surrounds the corona is called the perianth.

Features: white, yellow, peach, orange, pink or bicolored, spring flowers **Height:** 4–24"
Spread: 4–12" **Hardiness:** zones 3–9

Iris

Iris

*I*rises are steeped in history and lore. Many say the range of flower colors for bearded irises approximates that of a rainbow.

Growing

Irises prefer **full sun** but tolerate very light or dappled shade. The soil should be of **average fertility** and **well drained**. Japanese iris and Siberian iris prefer a moist but still well-drained soil.

Divide in late summer or early fall depending on the species. When dividing bearded iris rhizomes, replant with the flat side of the foliage fan facing the garden. Only replant clean, disease- and insect-free rhizomes.

Deadhead irises to keep them tidy.

Tips

All irises are popular border plants. Yellow and blue flag irises are also useful alongside streams or ponds. Dwarf cultivars make attractive additions to rock gardens.

Wash your hands after handling irises because they can cause severe internal irritation if ingested. You may not want to plant them close to places where children like to play.

Recommended

Many iris species and hybrids are available. Among the most popular is the bearded iris, often a hybrid of *I. germanica*. It has the widest range of flower colors. *I. cristata* (dwarf crested iris) is a low-growing native species that bears multi-colored blossoms. *I. pseudoacorus*

I. sibirica (above)
I. germanica 'Stepping Out' (below)

(yellow flag iris) is a water dweller and can tolerate those wet locations where little else thrives. *I. sibirica* (Siberian iris) offers assorted cultivars with flowers in a variety of shades, including purple, blue and white. *I. versicolor* (blue flag) produce blooms in shades of light to dark violet-blue but cultivars are also available in shades of red, pink, and reddish purple.

Ask for remontant (reblooming) iris cultivars for flowers in spring and again in the fall.

Features: spring, summer and sometimes fall flowers in almost every color combination including bicolored and multi-colored; attractive foliage **Height:** 4–48"
Spread: 6–48" **Hardiness:** zones 3–10

Magic Lily

Lycoris

L. squamigera (above)

espite its magical appearance, this perennial is also known as the spider lily, based on the outstretched stamens that resemble the legs of an arachnid. It is also known by other equally interesting names, including surprise lily, hurricane lily, naked lady and the resurrection lily.

Growing

Magic lily prefers to grow in locations with **full sun. Fertile, well-drained soil** is best. Mulching is recommended for moisture conservation.

The bulbs are best planted in late summer about 1' apart, with the bulb necks

The leaves remain green, adding interest in the winter landscape, only to die down to the ground while the plant goes into a dormant state. The leafless flower stalks emerge after the foliage has completely died down. Each stalk bears a cluster of blooms in late summer or early fall.

just above soil surface. To prevent rot, it's important to select an area for planting that remains drier during the bulbs' summer dormancy. Some water is tolerated if excellent drainage is available. Propagation by division should only take place once the plants have stopped blooming for the season.

Tips

Magic lily is ideal for sunny borders and rock gardens.

Recommended

L. squamigera is a cold-hardy bulbous perennial that forms clusters of funnel-shaped, pale rosy red flowers made up of slightly wavy tepals with curved tips. Long, wiry stamens emerge from the center of each fragrant flower. Strap-shaped leaves are produced each spring.

Features: unique, pinkish red flowers; form Height: 18–24" Spread: 12–18"
Hardiness: zones 6–10

Spring Star Flower

Ipheion

I. uniflorum 'Alba' (above), *I. uniflorum* (below)

What is more representative of a new spring season than a blooming, bulbous perennial with wildflower appeal? Spring star flower is unique and is deserving of wider use throughout the South.

Growing

Spring star flower grows well in **full sun to partial shade**. It performs well in almost any soil except those that are waterlogged.

Tips

Spring star flower is ideal for rock gardens and mixed beds and borders. As the perennials emerge and mature, the flowering and foliage of spring star flower begins to die back for the season. Plant spring star flower in groups around the base of larger growing perennials, including hostas, peonies and daylilies. It is also useful for naturalizing among grasses and woodlands.

Recommended

*I. **uniflorum*** is a vigorous, clump-forming perennial that emerges from a bulbous root. It produces narrow, strap-like foliage and single flowers with overlapping petals. The flowers are often a pale silvery blue. Many cultivars with scented, white, deep violet or lilac blue flowers are available at your local garden center.

The bulbs should be planted approximately 2" deep and apart from one another. Fall is the best time to plant, and division is unnecessary because the plants become more attractive as they multiply into larger clumps.

Features: starry-shaped, fragrant, colorful flowers; habit Height: 6–8" Spread: 4–6" Hardiness: zones 6–9

Tuberose

Polianthes

P. tuberosa (above & below)

Blooming usually takes place at the end of June and generally lasts for a few weeks with a possible second flush one or two months later in the season.

If you enjoy the heady fragrance of a summer bulb, then look no further. Tuberose has long been admired for its waxy white flowers and intoxicating scent.

Growing

Tuberose enjoys a **sunny**, warm but **sheltered** location in the garden. **Well-drained, moderately fertile soil** is best. The soil should be kept slightly moist throughout the winter dormant period. Propagation is possible by transplanting the bulblets in spring.

The bulbs should be covered with 2" of soil when planting and spaced approximately 6–8" apart from one another.

Tips

Tuberose is a great compliment to mixed borders that would benefit from a summer blooming cycle and a hit of scent. This tuberous perennial can also be grown in containers, both indoors and out, and the flowers are ideal for cutting and arrangements.

Recommended

*P. **tuberosa*** produces semi-upright, narrow leaves in a rosette form. Spikes of tubular, waxy, white flowers emerge from the rosette, emitting a heady, gardenia-like scent. A double cultivar is available with multi-layered petals. Each flower stem often produces an average of 30 flowers and can reach 3' heights or taller.

Features: fragrant, summer-blooming flowers
Height: 18–36" **Spread:** 24"
Hardiness: zones 7–10 with winter protection and when mulched; or treat as an annual

Chives
Allium

The delicate onion flavor of chives is best enjoyed fresh. Mix chives into dips or sprinkle them on salads and baked potatoes.

Growing

Chives grow best in **full sun**. The soil should be **fertile, moist** and **well drained,** but chives adapt to most soil conditions. These plants are easy to start from seed, but they do like the soil temperature to stay above 65° F before they germinate, so seeds started directly in the garden are unlikely to sprout before early summer.

Tips

Chives are decorative enough to be included in a mixed or herbaceous border and can be left to naturalize. In an herb garden, chives should be given plenty of space to allow self-seeding.

A. schoenoprasum (above & below)

Recommended

A. schoenoprasum forms a clump of bright green, cylindrical leaves. Clusters of pinkish purple flowers are produced in early and mid-summer. Varieties with white or pink flowers are available.

Chives spread recklessly as the clumps grow larger and the plants self-seed.

Chives are said to increase appetite and encourage good digestion.

Features: foliage; form; white, pink or pinkish purple flowers **Height:** 8–24" **Spread:** 12" or more **Hardiness:** zones 3–9

Coriander • Cilantro

Coriandrum

C. sativum (above & below)

The delicate, cloud-like clusters of flowers attract pollinating insects, such as butterflies and bees, as well as an abundance of predatory insects that help keep pest insects at a minimum in your garden.

Coriander is a multi-purpose herb—its leaves and seeds each have distinct flavors and culinary uses. The leaves are called cilantro and are used in salads, salsas and soups; the seeds are called coriander and are used in pies, chutneys and marmalades.

Growing

Coriander prefers **full sun** but tolerates partial shade. The soil should be **fertile, light** and **well drained**. This plant dislikes humid conditions and does best during a dry summer.

Tips

Coriander has pungent leaves and is best planted where people do not have to brush past it. It is, however, a delight to behold when in flower. Add a plant or two here and there throughout your borders and vegetable garden, both for the visual appeal and to attract beneficial insects. Coriander dies soon after it goes to seed, so sow several crops throughout spring to ensure you have leaves to harvest all summer long.

Recommended

C. sativum forms a clump of lacy basal foliage above which large, loose clusters of tiny, white flowers are produced. The seeds ripen in late summer and fall.

Features: form; foliage; white flowers; seeds
Height: 18–24" **Spread:** 8–18"
Hardiness: tender annual

Dill
Anethum

Dill leaves and seeds are probably best known for their use as pickling herbs, though they have a wide variety of other culinary uses.

Growing

Dill grows best in **full sun** in a **sheltered** location out of strong winds. The soil should be of **poor to average fertility, moist** and **well drained**. Sow seeds every couple of weeks in spring and early summer to ensure a regular supply of leaves. Dill should not be grown near fennel because they will cross-pollinate and the seeds of both plants will lose their distinct flavors.

Tips

With its feathery leaves, dill is an attractive addition to a mixed bed or border. It can be included in a vegetable garden but does well in any sunny location. It also attracts predatory insects to the garden.

Recommended

A. graveolens forms a clump of feathery foliage. Clusters of yellow flowers are borne at the tops of sturdy stems.

A. graveolens (above & below)

Dill turns up frequently in historical records as both a culinary and medicinal herb. It was used by the Egyptians and Romans and is mentioned in the Bible.

Features: feathery, edible foliage; yellow summer flowers; edible seeds **Height:** 24–60"
Spread: 12" or more **Hardiness:** annual

Lemon Balm

Melissa

M. officinalis (above & below)

The leaves can be harvested fresh or dried for teas, both hot and cold. They are also useful for flavoring desserts and savory dishes.

This lemon-scented and lemon-flavored herb is indispensable to cooks who love a touch of lemon in most dishes.

Growing

Lemon balm prefers to grow in **full sun** but grows quite successfully in locations with dappled shade. The soil should be **moist, fertile** and **well drained,** but this plant can tolerate poor, dry soils.

Taking cuttings for use encourages dense and vigorous growth. It's best to remove the flowers as they emerge.

Tips

Lemon balm may spread throughout your garden—after all, it is related to mint. Granted, lemon balm doesn't possess the same degree of invasiveness, but it may be best to prevent it from straying. Herb gardens are often the preferred location for this useful perennial, but it also works well as a fragrant filler in containers, mixed beds and borders.

Recommended

M. officinalis is a bushy, dense-growing perennial with roughly textured, hairy leaves that are fragrant and flavorful when bruised or crushed. Flowers are produced but are considered to be inconspicuous.

Features: fragrant, useful foliage **Height:** 24"
Spread: 18–24" **Hardiness:** zones 3–7

Mint
Mentha

The cool, refreshing flavor of mint lends itself to tea and other hot or cold beverages. Mint sauce, made from freshly chopped mint leaves, is often served with lamb.

Growing
Mint grows well in **full sun** or **partial shade**. The soil should be **average to fertile, humus rich** and **moist**. This plant spreads vigorously by rhizomes and may need a barrier in the soil to restrict its expansion.

Tips
Mint is a good groundcover for damp spots. It grows well along ditches that may only be periodically wet. It also can be used in beds and borders, but place mint carefully because it may overwhelm less vigorous plants.

The flowers attract bees, butterflies and other pollinators to the garden.

Recommended
There are many species, hybrids and cultivars of mint. Spearmint (**M. *spicata***), peppermint (**M. x *piperita***) and orange mint (**M. x *piperita citrata***) are three of the most commonly grown culinary varieties. There are also more decorative varieties with variegated or curly leaves as well as varieties with unusual, fruit-scented leaves.

M. x *piperita* 'Chocolate' (above)
M. x *piperita citrata* (below)

A few sprigs of fresh mint added to a pitcher of iced tea give it an extra zip.

Features: fragrant foliage; purple, pink or white summer flowers **Height:** 6–36"
Spread: 36"or more **Hardiness:** zones 4–8

Oregano · Marjoram
Origanum

O. vulgare 'Aureum' (above & below)

In Greek oros means 'mountain' and ganos means 'joy' or 'beauty,' so oregano translates as 'joy (or beauty) of the mountain.'

Oregano and marjoram are two of the best known and most frequently used herbs. They are popular in stuffings, soups and stews, and no pizza is complete until it has been sprinkled with fresh or dried oregano leaves.

Growing
Oregano and marjoram grow best in **full sun**. The soil should be of **poor to average fertility, neutral to alkaline** and **well drained**. The flowers attract pollinators to the garden.

Tips
These bushy perennials make a lovely addition to any border and can be trimmed to form low hedges.

Recommended
O. majorana (marjoram) is upright and shrubby with light green, hairy leaves. It bears white or pink flowers in summer and can be grown as an annual where it is not hardy.

O. vulgare var. *hirtum* (oregano, Greek oregano) is the most flavorful culinary variety of oregano. The low, bushy plant has hairy, gray-green leaves and bears white flowers. Many other interesting varieties of *O. vulgare* are available, including those with golden, variegated or curly leaves.

Features: fragrant foliage; white or pink summer flowers; bushy habit **Height:** 12–32" **Spread:** 8–18" **Hardiness:** zones 5–9

Parsley
Petroselinium

*A*lthough parsley is usually used as a garnish, it is rich in vitamins and minerals and is reputed to freshen the breath after garlic- or onion-rich foods are eaten.

Growing
Parsley grows well in **full sun** or **partial shade**. The soil should be of **average to rich fertility, humus rich, moist** and **well drained**. Direct sow seeds because the plants resent transplanting. If you start seeds early, use peat pots so the plants can be potted or planted out without disruption.

Tips
Parsley should be started where you mean to grow it, because it doesn't transplant well. Containers of parsley can be kept close to the house for easy picking. The bright green leaves and compact growth habit make parsley a good edging plant for beds and borders. It is also an excellent plant for butterfly gardens as a larval food source for swallowtails.

Recommended
P. crispum forms a clump of bright green, divided leaves. This plant is a biennial but is usually grown as an annual because the leaves are the desired parts, not the flowers or the seeds. Cultivars may have flat or curly leaves. Flat leaves are more flavorful and curly are more decorative. Dwarf cultivars are also available.

P. crispum (above), *P. crispum* var. *crispum* (below)

Parsley leaves make a tasty and nutritious addition to salads. Tear freshly picked leaves and sprinkle them over or mix them into your mixed greens.

Features: attractive foliage **Height:** 8–24"
Spread: 12–24" **Hardiness:** zones 5–8;
grown as an annual

Rosemary
Rosmarinus

R. officinalis (above & below)

To overwinter a container-grown plant, keep it in very light or partial shade outdoors in summer, then put it in a sunny window indoors for winter and keep it well watered but allow it to dry out slightly between waterings.

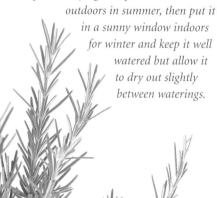

The needle-like leaves of rosemary are used to flavor a wide variety of culinary dishes, including chicken, pork, lamb, rice, tomato and egg dishes.

Growing
Rosemary prefers **full sun** but tolerates partial shade. The soil should be **well drained** and of **poor to average fertility**. These tender shrubs survive mild winters in Oklahoma, but to ensure their survival, they must be moved indoors.

Tips
Rosemary is often grown in a shrub border where hardy. In zones where rosemary is not hardy, it is usually grown in a container as a specimen or with other plants. Low-growing, spreading plants can be included in a rock garden or along the top of a retaining wall or can be grown in hanging baskets.

Recommended
R. officinalis is a dense, bushy evergreen shrub with narrow, dark green leaves. The habit varies somewhat between cultivars from strongly upright to prostrate and spreading. Flowers are usually in shades of blue, but pink-flowered cultivars are available. Cultivars are available that can survive in zone 6 in a sheltered location with winter protection. The plants rarely reach their mature size when grown in containers.

Features: fragrant, evergreen foliage; bright blue, or sometimes pink, summer flowers
Height: 8–48" **Spread:** 12–48"
Hardiness: zones 8–10

Sage
Salvia

Sage is perhaps best known as a flavoring for stuffing, but it has a great range of uses, and is often included in soups, stews, sausages and dumplings.

Growing

Sage prefers **full sun** but tolerates light shade. The soil should be of **average fertility** and **well drained**. These plants benefit from a light mulch of compost each year. They are drought tolerant once established.

Tips

Sage is an attractive plant for a border, adding volume to the middle of the border or as an attractive edging or feature plant near the front. Sage can also be grown in mixed planters.

Recommended

S. officinalis is a woody, mounding plant with soft, gray-green leaves. Spikes of light purple flowers appear in early and mid-summer. Many cultivars with attractive foliage are available, including the silver-leaved **'Berggarten,'** the purple-leaved **'Purpurea,'** the yellow-margined **'Icterina,'** and the purple, green and cream variegated **'Tricolor,'** which has a pink flush to the new growth.

S. officinalis 'Icterina' (above)
S. officinalis 'Purpurea' (below)

Sage has been used since at least ancient Greek times as a medicinal and culinary herb and continues to be widely used for both those purposes today.

Features: fragrant, decorative foliage; blue or purple summer flowers **Height:** 12–24"
Spread: 18–36" **Hardiness:** zones 5–8

Sweet Basil
Ocimum

The sweet, fragrant leaves of fresh basil add a delicious, licorice-like flavor to salads and tomato-based dishes.

Growing
Sweet basil grows best in a **warm, sheltered** location in **full sun**. The soil should be **fertile, moist** and **well drained**. Pinch the tips regularly to encourage bushy growth. Plant out or direct sow seed after frost danger has passed in spring.

Tips
Although sweet basil grows best in a warm spot outdoors in the garden, it can be grown successfully indoors in a pot by a bright window to provide you with fresh leaves all year.

Recommended
O. basilicum is one of the most popular of the culinary herbs. There are dozens of varieties, including ones with large or tiny, green or purple and smooth or ruffled leaves.

O. basilicum 'Genovese' (above & below)

Sweet basil is a good companion plant for tomatoes—both like warm, moist growing conditions and when you pick tomatoes for a salad you'll also remember to include a few sprigs or leaves of this aromatic and flavorful herb.

Features: fragrant, decorative leaves
Height: 12–24" **Spread:** 12–18"
Hardiness: tender annual

Athyrium
Athyrium

A. nipponicum 'Pictum' (above), A. felix-femina (below)

This genus of ferns includes some of the most well-behaved ferns; they add color and texture to shady spots without growing out of control.

Growing

Lady ferns and Japanese painted ferns grow well in **full, partial** or **light shade**. The soil should be of **average fertility, humus rich, acidic** and **moist**. Division is rarely required but can be done to propagate more plants.

Tips

Both ferns form an attractive mass of foliage, but they don't grow out of control like some ferns tend to. Include them in shade gardens and moist woodland gardens.

The colorful foliage of Japanese painted fern brightens up any shaded area with its metallic shades of silver, burgundy and bronze.

Recommended

A. filix-femina (lady fern) forms a dense clump of lacy fronds. It grows 12–24" tall and has a 24" spread. Cultivars are available, including dwarf cultivars and cultivars with variable foliage. **Subsp.** *asplenioides* (southern lady fern) is a native form with more triangular fronds.

A. niponicum var. *pictum* 'Metallicum' (Japanese painted fern) forms a clump of dark green fronds with a silvery or reddish metallic sheen. It grows 12–24" tall and has a 24" spread. Many cultivars are available. Some of the more colorful cultivars include **'Burgundy Lace,'** with metallic burgundy leaves; **'Pewter Lace,'** with fine, metallic gray foliage and **'Ursula's Red,'** with iridescent, silver-white and rich maroon-red leaves. (Zones 4–8)

Features: habit; foliage **Height:** 12–24"
Spread: 12–24" **Hardiness:** zones 3–8

Big Bluestem
Andropogon

This native grass is found growing naturally in almost every state and was historically a prominent part of the tall- and short-grass prairies. Although this plant is no longer as prevalent in its native habitat, its fine attributes will shine in any Oklahoma garden.

Growing
Big bluestem prefers to grow in **full sun**. The soil should be **light, low in fertility** or **poor** and **very well drained**. Excessive moisture can be a detriment to this plant.

This ornamental grass has a considerable tolerance for drought conditions. However, plants grown with little water often remain shorter in height and more compact in form than plants grown with adequate moisture.

Tips
The colorful foliage and flowerheads are a great compliment to the back of a mixed perennial and shrub border. Big bluestem also works well in a naturalized garden setting. This ornamental grass is an integral part of prairie grassland restorations.

Recommended
A. gerardii forms into a dense clump of arching, bluish green leaves that grow up to 5' in length or more and turn bronze in fall. Erect stems supporting deep red-purple flowers emerge in fall, followed by distinctive three-branched seedheads.

Features: colorful foliage, flowers and seedheads; form; habit **Height:** 4–6' **Spread:** 2–3' **Hardiness:** zones 4–10

Blue Oat Grass

Helictrotrichon

H. sempervirens (above & below)

This hardy grass is the perfect plant for those who desire a super-sized version of blue fescue for their garden.

Growing

Blue oat grass thrives in a **sunny** location. The soil should be **average to dry** and **well drained**. This grass is considered to be an evergreen but still needs a trim in spring to encourage new growth and to simply tidy it up.

Tips

This large, non-spreading grass is ideal for just about any setting because of its versatility. It works well in a water-wise design or a naturalized area. It is a lovely compliment to flowering perennials and shrubs because of its color, overall size and growth habit.

Recommended

H. sempervirens produces perfectly rounded, dome-shaped clumps of intensely blue, blade-like leaves. Wiry, tan stems tipped with tan seedheads emerge through the foliage.

Blue oat grass is easily propagated by division in early spring.

Features: brilliant blue foliage; decorative, spiked seedheads **Height:** 2–3'
Spread: 2–2$^1/_2$' **Hardiness:** zones 3–8

Blunt Lobed Wood Fern
Woodsia

W. obtusa (above & below)

This small, native fern is often found growing on rock ledges and cliffs throughout the eastern U.S. It is a perfect addition to a rock wall or rock garden, softening the appearance of hard edges.

Growing
Blunt lobed wood fern prefers **partial shade** and **fertile soil** that is **sharply drained** and **consistently moist**.

Tips
This fern species is ideal for woodland gardens, shade gardens and natural or introduced rocky outcrops, including rock gardens and rock walls.

The genus Woodsia *was named for Joseph Woods, a 19th-century architect and botanist.*

Recommended
W. obtusa is a small fern with deeply cut fronds that have a very lacy appearance. This species slowly creeps by rhizomes, ultimately reaching a spread of 18". It remains compact in a mounding form.

Although it is native to the U.S., this plant is listed as threatened in a number of states, including Maine and New Hampshire.

Also called: blunt-lobed woodsia
Features: ornate foliage; habit **Height:** 18–24"
Spread: 12–18" **Hardiness:** zones 4–10

Bugleweed

Ajuga

A. reptans 'Caitlin's Giant' (above & below)

Often labeled as a rampant runner, bugleweed grows best where it can roam freely. Although some species and cultivars are considered invasive in some states, well-behaved cultivars are available.

Growing

Bugleweed develops the best leaf color in **partial** or **light shade** but tolerates full shade. The leaves may become scorched when exposed to too much sun. Any **well-drained soil** is suitable. Divide these vigorous plants any time during the growing season. Remove any new growth or seedlings that don't show the hybrid leaf coloring.

Tips

Bugleweed makes an excellent groundcover for difficult sites, such as exposed slopes and dense shade. It is also attractive in shrub borders, where its dense growth prevents the spread of all but the most tenacious weeds.

Recommended

A. reptans is a low, quick-spreading groundcover. The many cultivars are grown for their colorful, often variegated foliage including **Burgundy Glow**, **Catlin's Giant** and **Variegata,** just to name a few.

Features: purple, blue, pink or white, late-spring to early-summer flowers; colorful foliage
Height: 3–6" **Spread:** 24–36"
Hardiness: zones 3–9

Christmas Fern

Polystichum

P. acrostichoides (above & below)

This genus of evergreen ferns provides greenery year-round, and the appearance of the fronds varies significantly from species to species.

Christmas fern is native to a large swath of the East Coast from Canada to Florida, and inland to the Mississippi River. Of the hardy ferns, it is one of the lower growing and less invasive plants.

Growing

Christmas fern grows well in **partial to full shade**. The soil should be **fertile, humus rich** and **moist**.

Divide this fern in spring to propagate more plants or to control its spread. Dead and worn-out-looking fronds should be removed in spring before the new ones fill in.

Tips

Christmas fern can be used in beds and borders and is a good choice for a shaded, pond-side garden. It is better suited to moist rather than wet conditions. The use of the fronds as Christmas decorations gave the plant its common name. Christmas fern is mostly deer proof.

Recommended

P. acrostichoides (Christmas fern) is a vase-shaped, evergreen, perennial fern that forms a circular clump of arching, dark green, lance-shaped fronds. Fertile fronds are shorter and slightly wider than the sterile fronds.

P. polyblepharum (Japanese tassel fern, bristle fern) is an evergreen species with 12–30" long, arching fronds. This ornate species can spread up to 3' wide. (Zones 5–8)

Features: evergreen foliage; easy to grow; problem free **Height:** 12–32" **Spread:** 18–36" **Hardiness:** zones 3–9

Cinnamon Fern

Osmunda

O. cinnamomea (above & below)

erns have a certain prehistoric mystique and can add a graceful elegance and textural accent to your garden.

Growing

Cinnamon ferns prefer **partial to light shade** but tolerate full sun if the soil is consistently moist. The soil should be **fertile, humus rich, acidic** and **moist**. Cinnamon ferns tolerate wet soil and will spread as offsets form at the plant bases.

Tips

These large ferns form an attractive mass when planted in large colonies. They can be included in beds and borders and make a welcome addition to a woodland garden or the edge of a pond.

The flowering fern's 'flowers' are actually its conspicuous, spore-producing sporangia.

Recommended

O. cinnamomea (cinnamon fern) has light green fronds that fan out in a circular fashion from a central point, with the whole plant resembling a large badminton birdie. Bright green, leafless, fertile fronds that mature to cinnamon brown are produced in spring and stand straight up in the center of the plant.

O. regalis (royal fern) forms a dense clump of foliage. Feathery, flower-like, fertile fronds stand out among the sterile fronds in summer and mature to a rusty brown.

Features: deciduous, perennial fern; decorative, fertile fronds; habit **Height:** 2–5'
Spread: 2–4' **Hardiness:** zones 3–9

Common Maidenhair Fern

Adiantum

A. pedatum (above & below)

Common maidenhair fern is often found growing in shady, moist locations beside streams or creeks. This non-invasive plant spreads slowly and looks wonderful planted with other shade-loving plants such as hosta, lungwort and toad lily.

Growing

Common maidenhair fern grows best in **partial to full shade** in **moist, well-drained, slightly acidic, fertile soil**.

Adiantum species have been used to cure bronchitis, coughs and asthma. They are also known as good hair tonics and restoratives.

Tips

Common maidenhair fern works best at the edge of a woodland garden. It makes a great addition to a shaded border or rock garden. This fern also does well in a streamside planting. When left to its own devices, common maidenhair fern spreads to form colonies.

This fern is easy to propagate in fall. Just slice off a section of the thick root mass and replant in a cool spot.

Recommended

*A. **pedatum*** is a deciduous, upright plant that bears branched, horizontally oriented, lance-shaped fronds and lobed, fan-shaped, mid-green foliage that turns yellow-green to yellow in fall. The leaflets have a waxy coating that rapidly sheds water and raindrops. The stems are dark brown to black.

Features: attractive foliage; growth habit; low maintenance **Height:** 12–24"
Spread: 12–24" **Hardiness:** zones 3–8

Creeping Phlox
Phlox

P. subulata (above & below)

Phlox comes in many shapes and sizes, from low creepers to tall, bushy border plants. Its fragrant flowers come in a range of colors with blooming times from early spring to mid-fall.

Growing
Most of the creeping phlox species and their cultivars are shade lovers. Their preferences can range from **partial to light** and even **full shade**. All like **fertile, humus-rich, moist, well-drained soil**. Divide in fall or spring.

Tips
The creeping species look good in rock gardens, at the front of borders or cascading over retaining walls.

Recommended
P. divaricata (blue phlox, woodland phlox) is a spreading, semi-evergreen perennial with lavender blue to pale purple or white flowers. Cultivars are available with cool-colored flowers in a wide range of tones.

P. stolonifera (creeping phlox) is a low, spreading plant that bears flowers in spring in several shades of purple.

P. subulata (moss phlox, moss pink) is very low growing and performs best in full sun. Its flowers come in various colors and blanket the evergreen foliage. A light shearing after the plant finishes flowering in June encourages tidy growth and possibly a second flush of flowers.

Features: white, blue, purple or pink, spring, summer or fall flowers **Height:** 2–14"
Spread: 12–20" **Hardiness:** zones 3–8

Dead Nettle

Lamium

L. maculatum 'White Nancy' (above), *L. maculatum* 'Beacon Silver' (below)

Dead nettle is a splendid shade groundcover. In flower it is wonderful, but the key to its value is its weaving mounds of fabulously attractive, variegated foliage.

Growing

Dead nettle prefers **partial to light shade** in **humus-rich, moist, well-drained soil** of **average fertility**. This plant grows vigorously in fertile soil. It is drought tolerant in the shade but can develop bare

patches if the soil is allowed to dry out for extended periods. Divide and replant in fall if bare spots become unsightly.

Dead nettle remains compact if sheared back after flowering. If it remains green over winter, shear it back in early spring.

Tips

This plant makes a useful groundcover for woodland or shade gardens. It works well under shrubs in a border, where it helps keep weeds down.

Recommended

L. maculatum (spotted dead nettle) is a low-growing, spreading species that has green leaves marked with white or silver. Many cultivars are available.

Features: white, pink or red-purple, spring or summer flowers; decorative, often variegated foliage **Height:** 8–10" **Spread:** 36" **Hardiness:** zones 3–8

Dryopteris

Dryopteris

*D*ryopteris species are reliable, hardy, tough and eye-catching ferns that are easy to grow.

Growing

Dryopteris species grow best in **partial shade** but tolerate full sun (with afternoon shade) in consistently moist soil. They also tolerate deep shade without much reduced vigor. The soil should be **fertile, humus rich, well-drained** and **moist**. Divide the plants in spring to control spread and to propagate.

Tips

These ferns are large and impressive in form. They are useful as specimens or grouped in a shaded area or a woodland garden. Dryopteris ferns are ideal additions to gardens that stay moist but not wet. They also beautifully complement other shade-loving plants, including hostas and coral bells.

Recommended

D. erythrosora is an upright, evergreen perennial fern with slightly arching, large, bronzy green to dark green fronds. The new growth has a bronzy red hue. An extreme, late frost will kill this fern to the ground, but the plant will recover and send up new growth.

D. erythrosora (above & below)

The genus Dryopteris *is made up of 225 species of moisture-loving, shady woodland ferns native to temperate regions around the world.*

Also called: Japanese red shield fern, wood fern **Features:** decorative fronds; habit; form; use **Height:** 2–3' **Spread:** 2–3' **Hardiness:** zones 5–9

Ebony Spleenwort
Asplenium

*F*inally, a fern that is truly drought-tolerant, durable and architectural in habit. The only thing this fern doesn't like is wet, poorly drained soil—otherwise it's a surefire winner.

Growing
Ebony spleenwort prefers **partial shade** in **humus-rich, moist** but **well-drained soil**. Divide in spring.

Tips
Woodland and partly shaded gardens are ideal locations for this fern. Once established, ebony spleenwort is able to support itself on its own, without a fuss, because of its drought-tolerant nature. It is guaranteed to thrive in dry shade under the canopy of other, larger plants, including trees.

Recommended
A. platyneuron is an evergreen species with narrow, fertile fronds that obscure the shorter, less-impressive sterile fronds. The fronds are a deep, dark green with dark stems.

Ebony spleenwort is a terrestrial fern. Terrestrial ferns are plants that grow on land as opposed to those that grow epiphytically, parasitically or aquatically.

Features: habit; drought-tolerance
Height: 16–18" **Spread:** 10–12"
Hardiness: zones 4–8

English Ivy
Hedera

One of the loveliest things about English ivy is the variation in green and blue tones it adds to the garden.

Growing

English ivy prefers **light or partial shade** but adapts to any light conditions from full sun to full shade. The soil should be of **average to rich fertility, moist** and **well drained**. The richer the soil, the better this vine grows. In a sunny, exposed site, the foliage can become damaged or dried out in winter.

Tips

Grown as a trailing groundcover, English ivy roots at the stem nodes. As a climbing vine, it clings tenaciously to house walls, tree trunks, stumps and many other rough-textured surfaces, and the rootlets can damage walls and fences. English ivy can be invasive in warm climates. For slower growth, choose small-leaved cultivars.

Recommended

H. helix is a vigorous plant with triangular, glossy, dark, evergreen leaves that may be tinged with bronze or purple in winter, thereby adding another season of interest to your garden. Many cultivars have been developed, including some with interesting, often variegated foliage. Check with your local garden center to see what is available.

H. helix (above & below)

English ivy is popular as a houseplant, and it is frequently used in wireframe topiaries.

Features: attractive foliage; climbing or trailing habit **Height:** 6–8" as a groundcover; up to 90' when climbing **Spread:** indefinite **Hardiness:** zones 5–9

Feather Reed Grass
Calamagrostis

C. x acutiflora 'Overdam' (above)
C. x acutiflora 'Karl Foerster' (below)

This is a graceful, metamorphic grass that changes its habit and flower color throughout the seasons. The slightest breeze keeps reed grass in perpetual motion.

Growing

Feather reed grass grows best in **full sun**. The soil should be **fertile, moist** and **well drained**. Heavy clay and dry soils are tolerated. Feather reed grass may be susceptible to rust in cool, wet summers or in areas with poor air circulation. Rain and heavy snow may cause it to flop temporarily, but it quickly bounces back. Cut it back to 4–6" in very early spring before growth begins, and divide it when it begins to die out in the center.

Tips

Whether it's used as a single, stately focal point, in small groupings or in large drifts, feather reed grass is a desirable, low-maintenance grass. It combines well with late-summer- and fall-blooming perennials.

Recommended

C. x *acutiflora* 'Karl Foerster' (Foerster's feather reed grass) is the most popular selection and forms a loose mound of green foliage from which airy bottlebrush flowers emerge in June. The flowering stems have a loose, arching habit when they first emerge but grow more stiff and upright over summer. Other cultivars include 'Overdam,' a compact, less hardy selection with white leaf edges. Watch for a new introduction called 'Avalanche,' which has a white center stripe.

Features: open habit becomes upright; silvery pink flowers turn rich tan; green foliage turns bright gold in fall; winter interest
Height: 3–5' **Spread:** 2–3'
Hardiness: zones 4–9

Fish-on-a-Fishing-Pole

Chasmanthium

This native grass is at home in moist, shady woodlands, and its bamboo-like foliage gives it a tropical flair.

Growing

Fish-on-a-fishing-pole thrives in **full sun to partial shade**, though it must stay moist in full sun to avoid leaf scorch, and its upright, cascading habit relaxes in deep shade. Soil should be of **average fertility** and **moist**, though dry soils are tolerated. This grass vigorously self-seeds, but the seedlings are easily removed and composted or shared with friends. Deadhead in fall to prevent seeds from germinating. Cut this plant back each spring to 2" above the ground.

C. latifolium (above & below)

Tips

These are tremendous plants for moist, shady areas. The plant's upright to cascading habit, especially when in full bloom, makes an attractive planting alongside a stream or pond, in a large drift or in a container.

The flower stalks, which resemble a string of dangling fish (hence the common name), can be pruned out to make interesting additions to fresh or dried arrangements.

Recommended

C. latifolium forms a spreading clump of unique, bright green, bamboo-like foliage. The scaly, dangling spikelet flowers arrange themselves nicely on delicate stems just slightly above the foliage. The foliage sometimes turns bronze, and the flowers turn gold in fall.

Also called: Indian wood oats, spangle grass, sea oats **Features:** bamboo-like foliage; unusual flowers; winter interest **Height:** 32"–4' **Spread:** 18–24" **Hardiness:** zones 5–8

Fountain grass
Pennisetum

P. setaceum 'Rubrum' (above & below)

Tips

Fountain grass can be used as an individual specimen plant or in group plantings and drifts, or it can be combined with flowering annuals, perennials, shrubs and other ornamental grasses. Annual selections are often planted in containers or beds for height and stature.

Recommended

Both perennial and annual fountain grasses exist. **P. alopecuroides**, is a popular perennial. This clumping species is one of the most reliable and showy of the ornamental selections. It bears glossy, bright green foliage 2–3' tall and wide. Cooler temperatures in fall bring out the streaked yellow and brown leaf variegations from base to tip. The foliage fades to a straw color in winter. Showy flowers emerge in summer and persist into fall. **P. setaceum** (annual fountain grass) has narrow green foliage and pinkish purple flowers that mature to gray. Its cultivar **'Rubrum'** (red annual fountain grass) has broader, deep burgundy foliage and pinkish purple sterile flowers.

*F*ountain grass' low-maintenance needs and graceful form make it easy to place. It softens any landscape, even in winter.

Growing

Fountain grass thrives in **full sun**. The soil should be of **average fertility** and **well drained**. Plants are drought tolerant once established. They may self-seed but are not troublesome. Shear back perennial selections in early spring, and divide them when they start to die out in the center.

Features: arching, fountain-like habit; silvery pink, dusty rose to purplish black foliage; white or pinkish purple flowers; winter interest
Height: 12–36" **Spread:** 12–36"
Hardiness: zones 6–10

Indian Grass

Sorghastrum

S. nutans (left & right)

Indian grass was once one of the most prevalent grasses of the tallgrass prairies throughout North America, but it has almost disappeared from the landscape except in Oklahoma. It has been designated the state grass of Oklahoma and is found in all of our 77 counties.

Growing

Indian grass prefers to grow in **full sun**. The soil should be **low to moderately fertile**, **well drained** and free of excessive winter moisture. Although tolerant of poor conditions and soil types, Indian grass prefers to grow in **deep, rich, moist, loamy soils**. This species is drought tolerant once established.

Tips

Indian grass can range in heights and spreads depending on the soil depth and level of moisture it's growing in, but it's often most effective in mass plantings and restoration sites or when naturalizing. It's also ideal for erosion control on slopes and provides a reliable show year-round, whether as a single specimen, a background grass or an accent to a mixed bed.

Recommended

S. nutans is a spreading perennial grass with a clumping form. It is upright in nature and bears foliage in shades of light to medium green and gray-green to pale shades of bluish green. The leaf blades are very narrow and gently arch out from the center. Yellowish tan flowers are borne in summer and are displayed as light, feathery plumes until the following spring. The foliage turns yellow to burnt orange in fall.

Features: reliability; habit; form; color
Height: 3–5' **Spread:** 2–3'
Hardiness: zones 4–9

Little Bluestem
Schizachyrium

S. scoparium (above)

Growing

Little bluestem requires **full sun** and is tolerant of almost any soil type except those with inadequate drainage. This ornamental plant is known to self-seed readily. Propagate by both seed and division.

Tips

Little bluestem is a welcome addition to xeriscape gardens and naturalized areas. It also works well in mixed borders and more contemporary settings.

Recommended

S. scoparium is a clumpforming grass. It produces light green, narrow blades 12–16" in length that become darker with maturity. The blade-like leaves are of a medium texture, somewhat hairy and soft to the touch. Flower spikes emerge through the foliage, supported by stems that rise high above the leaves. Decorative, fluffy plumes of ripening seedheads range in color from bronze to bright orange. '**Blaze**' is similar in form but displays more intense fall color, from reddish purples to orangy pinks.

ittle bluestem offers year-round interest. This ornamental grass has graceful, swaying blades in spring and summer, followed by tall flower spikes in summer that evolve into fluffy plumes of seedheads that catch the light.

Little bluestem is drought tolerant but benefits from a little summer watering in more arid regions.

Also called: prairie beard grass
Features: form; habit; decorative foliage and seedheads; winter interest **Height:** 2–4'
Spread: 1–3' **Hardiness:** zones 3–8

Maiden Grass

Miscanthus

*M*aiden grass is one of the most popular and majestic of all the ornamental grasses. Its graceful foliage dances in the wind and makes an impressive sight all year long.

Growing

Maiden grass prefers **full sun**. The soil should be of **average fertility**, **moist** and **well drained**, though some selections tolerate wet soil. All selections are drought tolerant once established. Leave the foliage in place to provide winter interest and then cut it back in spring before the new growth starts.

Tips

Give this magnificent beauty room to spread so you can fully appreciate its form. The plant's height will determine the best place for it in the border. Maiden grass creates a dramatic impact in groups or as a seasonal screen.

M. sinensis 'Strictus' (above)
M. sinensis 'Zebrinus' (below)

Recommended

There are many cultivars of **M. *sinensis***, all distinguished by the white midrib on the leaf blade. Some popular selections include **'Gracillimus'** (maiden grass), with long, fine-textured leaves; **'Grosse Fontaine'** (large fountain), a tall, wide-spreading, early-flowering selection; **'Morning Light'** (variegated maiden grass), a short, delicate plant with fine, white leaf edges; **var. *purpurescens*** (flame grass), with foliage that turns bright orange in early fall; **'Strictus'** (porcupine grass), a tall, stiff, upright selection with unusual horizontal yellow bands; and **'Zebrinus'** (zebra grass), an arching grass with horizontal yellow bands on the leaves.

Also called: eulalia, Japanese silver grass
Features: upright, arching habit; colorful summer and fall foliage; pink, copper or silver, late-summer and fall flowers; winter interest
Height: 4–8' **Spread:** 2–4'
Hardiness: zones 5–8; zone 4 with protection

Mondo Grass

Ophiopogon

O. planiscapus 'Nigrescens' (above)
O. japonicus 'Bluebird' (below)

Mondo grass is an excellent ground-cover, accent and contrast plant. The foliage displayed by black mondo grass is the perfect dark background to highlight any brightly colored plant or flower.

Growing

Mondo grass prefers to grow in **partial to light shade** in **moist, moderately fertile, well-drained, humus-rich soil.** The foliage is at its best in partial shade. Divide in

spring just as new growth resumes. This plant appreciates some winter protection of thick mulch in zones 5 and 6 but should otherwise be left uncovered. Foliage from the previous season should be removed before growth begins in early March.

Tips

Mondo grass can be used as a dense groundcover and for erosion control, because it spreads by rhizomes. Use it for border edges and containers.

Recommended

O. japonicus (mondo grass, monkey grass) produces dark green, grass-like foliage that grows 8–14" long and forms an evergreen mat of lush foliage, resembling an unkempt lawn. Short spikes of white, occasionally lilac-tinged flowers emerge in summer, followed by metallic blue fruit. Many cultivars are available in dwarf or variegated forms.

O. planiscapus 'Ebknizam' (EBONY NIGHT) (black mondo grass, black lily turf) has curving, almost black leaves and dark lavender flowers. It grows 4–6" tall and 6–12" wide. 'Nigrescens' has curving, almost black foliage and pink to white-flushed pink flowers. It grows 6–12" tall and 12" wide. Both cultivars produce blackish, berry-like fruit.

This plant is a member of the lily family and does not like being mowed.

Features: uniquely colored foliage; ground-cover habit; lavender, pink or white-flushed pink flowers **Height:** 4–12" **Spread:** 6–12" **Hardiness:** zones 5–9

Moneywort
Lysimachia

L. nummularia 'Aurea' (above and below)

Moneywort is a lovely, low-growing, ground-covering perennial prized for its colorful foliage.

Growing

Moneywort grows well in **light** or **partial shade**. The soil should be of **average fertility, humus rich** and **moist**. Divide this plant in spring or fall. The trailing stems can be cut back if they begin to spread farther than you would like.

Tips

An attractive and care-free addition to a moist border, moneywort is also a good plant to include in a rock garden, along a rock wall or in a container where the trailing stems have room to spread freely.

Recommended

*L. **nummularia*** is a prostrate, spreading plant with trailing stems. It bears bright yellow flowers in summer. A yellow-leaved cultivar, called '**Aurea**,' is popular and is frequently available.

Also called: creeping Jenny **Features:** yellow flowers; attractive foliage **Height:** 2–4"
Spread: 18" or more **Hardiness:** zones 2–8

Muhly Grass
Muhlenbergia

M. capillaris (above & below)

You may think you're witnessing some kind of unusual atmospheric phenomenon, when in fact it's the pinkish purple haze of the flower plumes borne from muhly grass. It's bound to have you wanting more.

Growing

Muhly grass thrives in bright, **sunny** locations in **well-drained, moist soil,** and it tolerates light shade. Once established, muhly grass prefers dryer soil that is **well aerated**; however, it is tolerant to just about any soil type.

Muhly grass is known to self-seed. If you want thicker stands, leave the ripened seedheads in place, allowing the seeds to fall, which results in a thicker, larger and denser clump of grass. Otherwise, remove the seed-heads before they ripen and fall.

Tips

This wild-looking, medium-sized grass is suited to mixed beds and borders with bolder-leaved plants that bring attention to its delicate appeal. It's also useful for naturalizing areas of your garden that require little attention or care and works well as a groundcover in areas with poor soil. The fall color stands out while most other plants look spent.

Recommended

M. capillaris (syn. *M. filipes;* gulf muhly-grass, mist grass, hairy awn muhly, pink muhlygrass, purple muhlygrass) produces a dense, knee-high stand of fine, wispy, grayish green grass. This showy clump can reach 3–4' heights and spreads. Purplish flowerheads emerge in late summer and last for up to two months. **'Regal Mist'** bears rosy pink flowers. **'White Cloud'** has white flowers.

M. lindheimeri (Lindheimer muhly) is a clumping grass bearing 12–18" tall, bluish green blades that gently arch toward the ground. Upright, spike-like flowers emerge in shades of purple from fall into winter and float 18–24" above the foliage.

Features: form; purple seedheads in fall
Height: 3–4' **Spread:** 3–4'
Hardiness: zones 5–10

Perennial Plumbago
Ceratostigma

C. plumbaginoides (above & below)

When you add this late-blooming, blue flower to the garden, take note of where you plant it. Because it is one of the last plants to shoot up new foliage in spring, you have to be careful not to plop another plant right on top of it.

Growing

Perennial plumbago grows best in **full sun** but survives with afternoon shade. It prefers **moist, well-drained soil** that is high in **organic matter**. Moderately drought tolerant once established, this quick-growing plant makes an excellent and tough groundcover. Divide in spring.

Tips

Perennial plumbago makes a wonderful addition to a rock garden, and it creeps happily between the rocks of a stone wall.

Recommended

C. plumbaginoides is a woody plant with erect stems. The foliage, which starts out light green highlighted with purple and becomes darker green as the outdoor temperature rises, turns bronzy red in fall.

Features: blue flowers; attractive habit; fall color **Height:** 7–12" **Spread:** 24–36"
Hardiness: zones 5–8

Sedge
Carex

C. comans 'Frosted Curls' (above)

Growing

Most sedges grow well in **full sun to partial shade** in **moist, well-drained, neutral to slightly alkaline soil**. 'Frosted Curls' prefers average to dry soil and is drought tolerant once established. Propagate by seed or division of clumps in mid-spring to early summer.

Tips

Use these plants in rock gardens, water features, containers and borders. The fine foliage of 'Frosted Curls' contrasts well with coarse-textured plants.

Stems can be cut to the ground in early spring before new growth occurs, or they can be 'combed' to remove the older foliage.

Recommended

There are many sedges available. *C. buchananii* (leatherleaf sedge) is a densely tufted, evergreen perennial with an arching habit and orange-brown foliage; *C. comans* 'Frosted Curls' (*C.* 'Frosted Curls'; New Zealand hair sedge) is a compact, clump-forming, evergreen perennial with fine-textured, very pale green, weeping foliage that appears almost iridescent and has unusual curled and twisted tips; *C. grayi* (Gray's sedge) has star-like seedheads and clumps of rich green leaves; *C. plantaginea* (seersucker sedge) has showy flowers and bright green leaves with many veins; *C. siderosticha* 'Variegata' (striped broad-leaved sedge) resembles a mass of narrow, 1" wide hosta leaves.

'Sedges have edges,' the opening line to a classic gardener's poem, points out that sedges, unlike true grasses, have triangular stems. Sedge foliage comes in green, blue, rust, bronze or gold, which allows the gardener to add broad strokes of color to the landscape.

Features: interesting, colorful foliage; growth habit **Height:** 6–36" **Spread:** 24–36" **Hardiness:** zones 5–9

Sensitive Fern

Onoclea

O. sensibilis (above & below)

A common sight along stream banks and in wooded areas in its native habitat, sensitive fern thrives in moist and shaded conditions.

Growing

Sensitive fern grows best in **light shade** but tolerates full or partial shade. The fronds can scorch if exposed to too much sun. The soil should be **fertile, humus rich** and **moist**, though some drought is tolerated. This plant is sensitive to frost and can be easily damaged by late and early frosts.

Tips

Sensitive fern likes to live in damp, shady places. Include it in shaded borders, woodland gardens and other locations with protection from the wind.

Recommended

O. sensibilis forms a mass of light green, deeply lobed, arching fronds. Fertile fronds are produced in late summer and persist through winter. The spores are produced in structures that look like black beads, giving the fertile fronds a decorative appearance that makes them a popular addition to floral arrangements.

Features: deciduous, perennial fern; attractive foliage; habit **Height:** 24"
Spread: indefinite **Hardiness:** zones 4–9

Southern Wood Fern
Thelypteris

T. kunthii (above & below)

This lovely fern spreads quickly and is useful for filling lightly shaded locations.

Ferns generally prefer the shadier parts of a garden, but southern wood fern is not only tolerant of the sun but thrives in the heat and in sunnier locations.

Growing
Southern wood fern grows well in **light** or **partial shade** but can tolerate full sun as long as the soil remains moist. The soil should be of **average fertility, humus rich, slightly acidic** and **moist**. This fern grows adequately in hot, dry conditions but is most impressive in moist, shaded locations.

Divide the plants regularly or pull up extra plants to control the vigorous spread. Cut out crusty old foliage in spring before new growth begins.

Tips
This fern makes an attractive addition to a shaded garden or to the edge of a woodland garden. It is best used where there is plenty of room for it to spread.

Recommended
*T. **kunthii*** (*T. normalis*) is a deciduous, perennial fern that spreads by rhizomes and spores. Where it is happy, it spreads quickly. This fern has large, triangle-shaped, gently arching, light green fronds and white stems. The fronds are not frost hardy.

Also called: Kunth's maiden fern, southern shield fern, widespread maiden fern
Features: foliage; fast growth; easy to maintain
Height: 12–36" **Spread:** 24–48"
Hardiness: zones 7–10

Strawberry Geranium

Saxifraga

S. *stolonifera* 'Kinki Purple' (above), S. *stolonifera* (below)

More than 400 species of *Saxifraga* are known, but S. *stolonifera* is probably one of the best selections for Oklahoma because of its growth and flowering habits and its tolerance for excessive heat.

Growing

Strawberry geranium prefers **partial to full shade**. The soil should be **neutral to alkaline, fertile, moist** and **well drained**. Divide in spring.

Tips

Strawberry geranium is an excellent addition to rock gardens and borders but also works well in shaded, mixed borders. It can also be used as a groundcover in moist soil.

Also called: strawberry begonia, mother of thousands **Features:** white summer flowers; attractive foliage; spreading habit
Height: 12–24" **Spread:** 24"
Hardiness: zones 7–9

Recommended

S. ***stolonifera*** produces a thick, semi-evergreen mat of attractively gray-veined leaves with purple undersides, along with spikes of tiny, white flowers. The parent plant sends out shoots, at the ends of which grow tiny new plants.

This perennial groundcover is neither a begonia nor a geranium, but it displays physical characteristics reminiscent of both.

Switch Grass

Panicum

P. virgatum cultivar (above)
P. virgatum 'Heavy Metal' (below)

Switch grass' delicate, airy panicles fill gaps in the garden border and can be cut for fresh or dried arrangements.

A native to the prairie grasslands, switch grass naturalizes equally well in an informal border and a natural meadow.

Growing

Switch grass thrives in **full sun, light shade** or **partial shade**. The soil should be of **low fertility** and **well drained**, though this grass adapts to moist or dry soils and tolerates conditions ranging from heavy clay to lighter sandy soil. Cut switch grass back to 4–6" from the ground in early spring. The flower stems may break under heavy, wet snow or in exposed, windy sites.

Tips

Plant switch grass singly in small gardens or in large groups in spacious borders or at the edges of ponds or pools for a dramatic, whimsical effect. The seedheads attract birds, and the foliage changes color in fall, so place this plant where you can enjoy both features.

Recommended

P. virgatum (switch grass) is suited to wild meadow gardens. Some of its popular cultivars include **'Heavy Metal'** (blue switch grass), an upright plant with narrow, steely blue foliage flushed with gold and burgundy in fall; **'Prairie Sky'** (blue switch grass), an arching plant with deep blue foliage; and **'Shenandoah'** (red switch grass), small, compact selection with red-tinged, green foliage that turns burgundy in fall.

Features: clumping habit; green, blue or burgundy foliage; airy panicles of flowers; fall color; winter interest **Height:** 3–5'
Spread: 30–36" **Hardiness:** zones 3–9

Vinca

Vinca

Vinca grows well in a wide range of soils and welcomes spring with a bounty of blue flowers.

Growing

Vinca grows well in **partial to full shade. Moist, well-drained soil** of any type will do. After planting, mulch the soil with shredded leaves and compost to keep the soil moist and to prevent weeds from sprouting up while vinca fills in.

Tips

Vinca is a useful, attractive groundcover in a shrub border, under trees or on a shady bank. This plant is shallow-rooted and can out-compete weeds without interfering with deeper-rooted shrubs. Shear it back in early spring if it begins to outgrow its space.

V. minor (above & below)

Recommended

*V. **minor*** forms a low, loose mat of trailing stems. Purple or blue flowers are borne in a flush in spring and sporadically throughout summer. Many cultivars are available with different-colored flowers or variegated foliage.

The Romans used the long, trailing stems of vinca to make wreaths. This use of the plant may explain its name, which is derived from the Latin vincire, *'to bind.'*

Also called: myrtle, lesser periwinkle
Features: blue, purple, white or red, mid-spring to fall flowers; trailing habit **Height:** 4–8"
Spread: indefinite **Hardiness:** zones 4–8

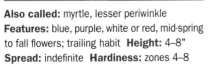

Virginia Chain Fern
Woodwardia

W. virginica

Virginia chain fern is almost always found in or around sheltered, damp places in warmer parts of the world including North America. Do you have such a place in your garden?

Growing
Virginia chain fern thrives in **partially shaded** areas, in **moderately fertile, neutral soil** that is **consistently moist** if not wet.

Tips
Moisture is an important factor for this fern's success. Locations surrounding water features including ponds and streams are best, unless the shaded area is very well mulched to maintain the moisture levels in the soil. Woodland settings also work well.

Recommended
W. virginica is a slow-spreading fern that is often mistaken for a cinnamon fern (*Osmunda cinnamomea*) owing to similar fronds, leaf placement and overall habit. The fronds can reach 3–4' lengths and 8–10" widths. This species grows into a dense clump of foliage with dark purple-brown stems.

The name 'chain fern' refers to the parallel, chain-like rows of spores on the undersides of the leaves.

Features: reliability, dense habit, form
Height: 3–4' **Spread:** 2–3'
Hardiness: zones 3–10

Glossary

Acidic soil: soil with a pH lower than 7.0

Annual: a plant that germinates, flowers, sets seed and dies in one growing season

Alkaline soil: soil with a pH higher than 7.0

Basal foliage: leaves that form from the crown, at the base of the plant

Bract: a modified leaf at the base of a flower or flower cluster

Corm: a bulb-like, food-storing, underground stem, resembling a bulb without scales

Crown: the part of the plant at or just below soil level where the shoots join the roots

Cultivar: a cultivated plant variety with one or more distinct differences from the species, e.g., in flower color or disease resistance

Deadhead: to remove spent flowers to maintain a neat appearance and encourage a longer blooming season

Direct sow: to sow seeds directly in the garden

Dormancy: a period of plant inactivity, usually during winter or unfavorable conditions

Double flower: a flower with an unusually large number of petals

Espalier: a tree trained from a young age to grow on a single plane—often along a wall or fence

Genus: a category of biological classification between the species and family levels; the first word in a scientific name indicates the genus

Grafting: a type of propagation in which a stem or bud of one plant is joined onto the rootstock of another plant of a closely related species

Hardy: capable of surviving unfavorable conditions, such as cold weather or frost, without protection

Hip: the fruit of a rose, containing the seeds

Humus: decomposed or decomposing organic material in the soil

Hybrid: a plant resulting from natural or human-induced cross-breeding between varieties, species or genera

Neutral soil: soil with a pH of 7.0

Offset: a horizontal branch that forms at the base of a plant and produces new plants from buds at its tips

Panicle: a compound flower structure with groups of flowers on short stalks

Perennial: a plant that takes three or more years to complete its life cycle

pH: a measure of acidity or alkalinity; the soil pH influences availability of nutrients for plants

Rhizome: a root-like, food-storing stem that grows horizontally at or just below soil level, from which new shoots may emerge

Rootball: the root mass and surrounding soil of a plant

Seedhead: dried, inedible fruit that contains seeds; the fruiting stage of the inflorescence

Self-seeding: reproducing by means of seeds without human assistance, so that new plants constantly replace those that die

Semi-double flower: a flower with petals in two or three rings

Single flower: a flower with a single ring of typically four or five petals

Species: the fundamental unit of biological classification; the entity from which cultivars and varieties are derived

Standard: a shrub or small tree grown with an erect main stem, accomplished either through pruning and training or by grafting the plant onto a tall, straight stock

Sucker: a shoot that comes up from the root, often some distance from the plant; it can be separated to form a new plant once it develops its own roots

Tender: incapable of surviving the climatic conditions of a given region and requiring protection from frost or cold

Tuber: the thick section of a rhizome bearing nodes and buds

Variegation: foliage that has more than one color, often patched or striped or bearing leaf margins of a different color

Variety: a naturally occurring variant of a species

Index of Recommended Species Plant Names

Entries in **bold** type indicate the main plant species; *italics* indicate botanical names.

Plantain lily. *See* Hosta
Polianthes, 130
Polygonatum, 67
Polystichum, 146
Porcelain berry, 118
Portulaca, 35
President Lincoln. *See* Mister
 Lincoln
Ptelea, 87
Pulmonaria, 60

Quercus, 93

Redbud, 94
 Chinese
 eastern
Rose mallow. *See* Hardy
 hibiscus
Rose Moss, 35
 moss rose, 35
 ornamental purslane, 35
Rosemary, 138
Rose-of-Sharon, 95
Rosmarinus, 138
Rudbeckia, 41
Russian sage, 64

Sacred bamboo. *See* Nandina
Sage (annual). *See* Salvia
Sage (herb), 139
Sage (perennial). *See*
 Artemisia
Sage. *See* Perennial salvia
Salvia, 139
Salvia, 36
 blue sage, 36
 mealy cup sage, 36
 scarlet sage, 36
 Texas sage, 36
Salvia, 63
Saxifraga, 167
Scabiosa, 34
Scaevola, 20
Scarlet bush. *See* Firebush
Schizachyrium, 158
Sea oats. *See* Fish-on-a-
 fishing-pole
Sedge, 164
 Gray's, 164
 leatherleaf, 164

New Zealand hair sedge,
 164
 seersucker, 164
 striped broad-leaved, 164
Sedum, 68
Sempervivum, 55
Sensitive fern, 165
Shasta daisy, 65
Shrub verbena. *See* Lantana
Smoke tree, 96
Smokebush. *See* Smoke tree
Sneezeweed, 66
Solenostemon, 17
Solidago, 53
Soloman's Seal, 67
Sorghastrum, 157
Southern shield fern. *See*
 Southern wood fern
Southern wax myrtle, 97
Southern wood fern, 166
Spangle grass. *See* Fish-on-
 a-fishing-pole
Spider flower. *See* Cleome
Spiraea, 98
Spirea, 98
 bridalwreath, 98
 Japanese, 98
 Vanhoutte, 98
Spring star flower, 129
Stachys, 57
Star cluster. *See* Pentas
Stonecrop, 68
Strawberry begonia. *See*
 Strawberry geranium
Strawberry geranium, 167
Strobilanthes, 31
Stylophorum, 46
Summer snapdragon. *See*
 Angelonia
Summersweet clethra. *See*
 Sweet pepper shrub
Swallow-wort. *See* Tropical
 butterfly weed, 37
Sweet basil, 140
Sweet pepper shrub, 99
Sweet pepperbush. *See*
 Sweet pepper shrub
Sweetspire. *See* Sweet
 pepper shrub
Switch grass, 168

 blue, 168
 red, 168

Taxodium, 72
Tecoma, 38
Thelypteris, 166
Thuja, 71
Thunbergia, 112
Tickseed. *See* Lanceleaf
 coreopsis
Toad lily, 69
Tricyrtis, 69
Tropical butterfly weed, 37
Tropical milkweed. *See*
 Tropical butterfly weed
Tuberose, 130

Ulmus, 80

Veronicastrum, 51
Vinca, 169
Viola, 29
Virginia chain fern, 170
Virginia creeper, 119
 woodbine, 119
Vitex, 75

Widespread maiden fern.
 See Southern wood fern
Winter Jasmine, 100
Wisteria, 120
 American, 120
 Kentucky, 120
Wood fern. *See* Dryopteris
Woodsia, 144
Woodwardia, 170
Wormwood. *See* Artemisia

X Chitalpa, 77

Yarrow, 70
 common, 70
Yellow bells, 38

Zinnia, 28

Author Biographies

Steve Owens is an Oklahoma horticulturist and plantsman with over 20 years of professional horticultural experience. His love of gardening began early, inspired by his father and grandfather in rural Sequoyah County.

Steve graduated from Vian High School and later earned both Bachelors and Masters degrees in horticulture from Oklahoma State University. Since 2001, Steve has been the writer, producer and host of *Oklahoma Gardening*, a 30-minute, award-winning television program that airs weekly on OETA (Oklahoma Educational Television Authority). The program reaches an estimated 175,000 viewers throughout Oklahoma and portions of neighboring states.

In 2006, Steve was bestowed the George J. Vaclavek Gold Medal from the Oklahoma Horticultural Society. Although he is interested in all aspects of gardening, he has a great love of garden design, native plants, perennials and heat-tolerant flowering tropical plants and vines. Steve lives, works and gardens in Stillwater.

Laura Peters is a certified Master Gardener with 23 gardening books to her credit. She has gained valuable experience in every aspect of the horticultural industry in a career that has spanned more than 18 years. She enjoys sharing her practical knowledge of organic gardening, plant varieties and gardening products with fellow gardeners.

Acknowledgments

I would like to thank Laura Peters and Lone Pine Publishing for the opportunity to assist in creating this book. The experience has been exciting, engaging and lots of fun. I would also like to thank the many gardeners of Oklahoma who have, through the years, allowed me to visit and admire their wonderful gardens. Special thanks to Ruth, my wife and best friend. —*Steve Owens*

A big thanks to my parents, Gary and Lucy Peters, and my friends for their endless encouragement and support all these years. I would also like to thank Steve Owens for his hard work and immense knowledge of everything Oklahoma. Lastly, thanks to all the people who allowed me to photograph their gardens. Without you, this book would have been a lot less fun and colorful. Happy gardening! —*Laura Peters*